SO WHO'S PERFECT!

D0369755

Dhyan Cassie

So Who's Perfect!

People with visible differences tell their own stories

Foreword by Dean A. Bartel

HERALD PRESS
Scottdale, Pennsylvania
Kitchener, Ontario
1984

362.4092
Cas

Library of Congress Cataloging in Publication Data

Cassie, Dhyan.
  So who's perfect!

  1. Physically handicapped—United States—Biography.
I. Title.
HV3012.C37   1984   362.4'092'2[B]   84-12948
ISBN 0-8361-3372-2 (pbk.)

SO WHO'S PERFECT!
Copyright © 1984 by Herald Press, Scottdale, Pa. 15683
    Published simultaneously in Canada by Herald Press,
    Kitchener, Ont., N2G 4M5. All rights reserved.
Library of Congress Catalog Card Number: 84-12948
International Standard Book Number: 0-8361-3372-2
Printed in the United States of America
Design by David Hiebert

90 89 88 87 86 85 84 10 9 8 7 6 5 4 3 2 1

*For those who shared their lives
and taught me more than I
could ever learn in
a textbook.*

CONTENTS

FOREWORD

So Who's Perfect! could be a book about all of us—our hopes, our fears, our frustrations, and our sensitivities.

It is a book of life experiences as told by persons who daily live with significant handicaps. That makes it unique because most of us do not really know what it's like to face constant physical and attitudinal barriers.

It is not easy to be patently able-bodied in the presence of someone with an obvious disability. We suddenly realize how handicapped we all are because we don't know how to respond.

Dhyan Cassie presents these firsthand accounts without analysis or editorial comment. You may be surprised at the honesty of expression, moved by the deep wounds—to use Jean Vanier's term—some persons have experienced, and intrigued by the way some have learned to cope.

I challenge readers to suspend judgment when reading these accounts. Forget your stereotypes and preconceptions. Just listen with your heart and mind.

This book confirms what I have come to know about many persons with disabilities. They want to be treated like everybody else—not as special or different. They want the same opportunities for employment, recreation, socializing, and family life.

The myth that most persons with disabilities want to be with "their own kind" is challenged. Most see a mainstreamed education approach as desirable. Bob, who has spina bifida and went to a special school says, "Once you're put in an environment that's handicapped, it's like you're in a rut and can't get out."

Paul, who is missing an arm due to cancer, says, "I just want to be with normal people." That does not seem too much to ask. Yet every day we put up barriers to keep the Bobs and Pauls of this world out of our circle.

We shut them out with architectural barriers, with our language which labels and categorizes, with pity instead of compassion, and with segregated housing and schools instead of integration. But mostly we shut them out with our attitudes and insensitivity to their needs.

Persons with disabilities, just like other people, have struggles with self-acceptance and not wanting to ask for help. I was struck as I read their stories how much we have in common.

Common advice offered to all those who want to play Boy Scout or Florence Nightingale is to ask first. It is quite disconcerting to suddenly have someone grab your arm or push your wheelchair without inquiring if assistance is desired.

Several years ago I was with a friend who uses a wheelchair. I offered to help him up an eight-inch curb. He politely refused and proceeded to maneuver up the curb himself. He was more able than I had assumed.

Don't stare! Our lack of awareness causes us to turn our head and embarrass ourselves and the person who appears different. It is a reminder of how segregated our lives have become and how seldom we have opportunity to rub shoulders with persons who are disabled. Sincere inquiries into the nature of the person's condition are usually welcome, but not the cold inquisitive gaze.

How then should we respond and what can we learn? These stories will give you new insight on how to interact and be supportive of persons with visible differences without being paternalistic. You will discover their insights about God and the effect their disability has on their relationship with him.

Judith, a woman who stutters, summed up the sentiment of many about God with her statement, "I believe God allows us to have problems for purposes of instruction in this life."

In my work with parents of mentally handicapped children, I have found they often have difficulty accepting God's benevolence in this situation. For the parents there is often a sense of guilt over having a child with a disability.

We all have a place in God's created world. It is up to each of us to help the other find that place in life where our abilities and gifts are recognized and can be used. We are responsible for each other. And we are to model and foster acceptance. I am only as important as I allow you to be.

These personal stories will change how you think about persons with disabilities or differences, if you allow your own attitudes to be challenged.

If you are a professional worker in disabilities, this book will broaden your understandings and insights. If you are a person with a disability, you may find comfort in the shared experiences.

If you are a teacher, this book will help you enlighten your students about disabling conditions. If you are a pastor, read it and recommend it to your parishioners as a window into God's beautiful and wonderful creation.

—Dean A. Bartel
Consultant in Developmental Disabilities
Elkhart, Indiana

AUTHOR'S PREFACE

I had taught the deaf for three years before I met Laurel Raci, a deaf adult who was my teaching assistant. She poured out her story until I began to understand deafness—not textbook style, but real-life, what-it-means-to-be-deaf style. Then I learned to teach. I wondered how much time has been wasted, how many hurts have been inflicted by well-meaning people who have never heard the stories of those with whom they work and live.

My husband, a Presbyterian minister, has had people with visible or physical differences in his congregations, and yet the subject has been avoided. Aren't we to minister to the whole person? Transportation systems are devised, schools established, buildings constructed without consulting the real "experts." Why do we avoid hearing the stories that are ready to be told?

I dreamed of interviewing people with visible and physical differences for ten years. I mentioned my idea to Rachel Hyman, speech and language pathologist, friend and co-worker. She offered to help. We sat down and wrote out a list of the "differences" we would like to cover.

I called the school for the blind and asked the receptionist if she knew a blind adult we could interview. Lucy Boyle said, "Why not me!" and she invited me to her home. That was easy!

I saw Ken in the grocery store, a handsome young man with a birthmark splashed across his face. Not so easy! With knees quaking, I walked over to him. "I see you have a birthmark. May I interview you for a book?" Waiting for the blow, I was overwhelmed to hear, "Sure. When? Here's my address. Come on over."

I work as an audiologist in a rehabilitation center and am on a task force on the disabled for the Presbytery of Philadelphia so I am personally acquainted with many handicapped people. They were unhesitating in their sharing. But how could I interview people I didn't even know? I approached some of my subjects on the street. The answer was almost always the same. "Sure!" In my car I chased a jogger the wrong way down a one-way street until I got his attention. Standing panting in his red jogging suit grinning under his completely hairless scalp, he said, "Sure you can interview me, but what's so different about me?"

Was anyone offended? I don't think so. Many expressed Pat's feelings when she said, "I've always felt I had a story to tell." The most sensitive were the overweight. It was a surprise to discover how socially discriminated against they are.

A few of my subjects did not need to be approached—they offered themselves. I sat next to a lovely lady at a conference and was describing my book to her. "Why don't you interview me?" she offered. "Your readers might find albinism interesting."

Al with alopecia, was at the public library sporting a T-shirt that read, "God made only a few perfect heads. On the others he put hair."

The tape recorder was a necessity, but an enemy. I had all the problems of a novice—dead batteries, short cords, static, background noise. Transcribing was accomplished with one ear flat against the recorder while writing out page after page. Then there was cutting, pasting, arranging, typing. How many times did I hear, "You should have a word processor." I know. But I didn't.

This book progressed from "idea" to "fact" through my friend Rachel Hyman, who said, "Let's do it!" and proceeded to help outline, interview, and transcribe. My daughter Andrea, son Giles, and their friends offered constructive criticism. My husband never tired in reading and enthusiastically endorsing the work. Barbara Niebruegge helped to edit the book. Helen Staubach provided publicity material, sharing her professional knowledge of publishing. Jack McCloskey, a subject in the book, devised the title. Friends at work patiently, if helplessly, listened to the unfolding drama.

The results were worth the struggle. The stories unfolded with great pathos, beauty, humor, compassion, and understanding. Most of the people I interviewed I will never see again, but they are my friends—and yours.

—Dhyan Cassie
Lansdowne, Pennsylvania

1. INTRODUCTION

*Adversities do not make the
man either weak or strong, but
they reveal what he is.*
—Faith Forsyte, Tit-Bits

*The facts of existence are like so
much loose type which can be
set up into many meanings. One
man leaves these facts in chaotic
disarrangement, or sets them
into cynical affirmations, and he
exists. But another man takes
the same facts and by spiritual
insight makes them mean glo-
rious things and he lives indeed.*
—Harry Emerson Fosdick

This book is about people who have visible differences—people who have to prove themselves before they begin, who have to be more forgiving, more loving, more fun, more intelligent, and more outgoing than those who fit into the mainstream of society. It is about people who bear the scars of childhood, when taunting and isolation are accepted as some fault of their own. It is about teenage years when it is imperative to be a clone to every other teenager.

It is about the persistence and bravery of people like Kenneth, who contends with a birthmark on his face. "When I got into high school, I decided I was not going to be the gopher. I was going to stand up for myself," he says. Or Suzanne, with muscular dystrophy, who had to force herself to be outgoing in college. "You can change what goes on out there, if you just force yourself to." And it goes on into job-seeking years, family rearing time, and the peace of maturity.

This book is designed for teachers, parents, co-workers, friends, and casual acquaintances to assist them in removing the barriers to true education, friendship, and respect with persons who have handicaps or are visibly different from others. We have related to these persons on our best instincts, but have often inflicted needless hurts and hardships. Presuming to know what is best is an indulgence we can no longer afford. The visibly different are not hidden nor mute. They are in the offices, the unemployment lines, at the computers, and in the schools. And it is not only they who are being deprived by unconscious barriers. "All those prejudices I could do without. Not only did society's stumbling blocks deprive me, but let's be grand about it—they deprived society" (Bern).

People with visible handicaps are being catapulted into the mainstream of schools and society—often faster than we are learning to accommodate them. With a surprising unanimity of opinion, the men and women interviewed do not want to be segregated, insulated, or separated by being in "handicapped groups." They feel they must prove themselves with nondisabled people.

Suzanne, with muscular dystrophy, went to a school for "crippled children." She felt it was "too much of an isolating experience. I had nothing in common with these people except they were disabled." Her solution? "You've got to mainstream kids from kindergarten on. You get the normal exposed to the ones with disabilities and they're not going to be afraid of people with disabilities anymore."

Bob, with spina bifida, reiterated this point of view. "It would have been better if I had been with ambulatory children. Once you're put in an environment that's handicapped, it's like you're in a rut and you can't get out of it." Into adulthood, they do not want to be grouped with other disabled people. Jan being partially sighted felt she had not proven her own worth until she had worked with sighted people. Now that she has had that experience, she is content working with the blind.

Paul, missing an arm said, "I'm not involved in going to any handicapped groups. I just want to be healthy." This is not to denigrate necessary support groups such as the multiple sclerosis group that Al attends, but to point out the need to open all avenues of activity. Pat, with cerebral palsy, was asked to be vice-president of an advocacy group. "They weren't disabled people. Vice-president! It blew my mind!"

Those with sensory handicaps—the deaf, hard of hearing, blind and partially sighted—relate divergent experiences and opinions concerning education. Lucy, who was born blind, is grateful she went to a school for the blind. She believes it would have been too much to struggle with blindness while coping with the everyday problems of going to school. Eric hated going away from home to a school for the deaf and yet, he feels it is better to live in a residential school. "You learn more." However, George, after becoming blind at the age of eighteen asserts that he tends toward mainstreaming because "the intelligent handicapped students are going to get a better deal out of life." Administrators, educators, and parents struggle with the questions—who should be mainstreamed into the schools and at what age? People who have been through the system and are now facing adulthood share with us experiences that will be helpful in making these decisions.

All those with sensory handicaps stressed that they want to be treated as individuals. "The one thing that bothers me most in the whole world is being treated as if we are different because we are handicapped. We are different because we are different individuals" (Lucy). "She's Susan, not blind Susan," Jack speaks of his wife. Gene repeats, "A person ought to be treated as an individual and not be given exclusionary treatment or overly inclusive treatment. He should be given an opportunity to be a human being."

The visibly different are not all physically handicapped but may be handicapped socially by their difference from the norm in size, facial appearance, speech, or age. In some ways, social mainstreaming is more difficult than physical mainstreaming, for no special provisions are made for those with birthmarks, scars, keloids, or for those who stutter or cannot remember words, or for those who are overweight, short, or tall. Society has not been made sensitive to these visibly different, for they have no group, no spokespersons—they fend for themselves, often feeling embarrassed, ashamed, inferior.

Mildred, with a birthmark covering the side of her face, declares, "It is a tempering of the sword through the entire life." Rebecca, fifteen years old, also has a birthmark on her face and her mother shares, "If you yourself have never been with anyone who has been stared at constantly, then you don't know how it is. In war, men need courage once, but hers is needed every day."

Judith, who is beautiful and intelligent, stutters. "School was terrible. Kids and adolescents are not comfortable with those who are not like them—those they know they can hurt." Peter, who is short, says, "People discount me because I'm short and they say, 'Oh, you can't be serious!'" Bonnie, overweight, never had a date in high school. She was brought up feeling that fat was first and person was second, so the person got lost in the fat. Jan had an inferiority complex due to her albinism. "I think it's this old thing Americans have about differences. Any difference has to be a bad difference." Our frame of reference needs to be broadened.

Several people were interviewed who became visibly different in adulthood due to accident, sickness, or age. A different type of adjustment is made. "It's an evolutionary process," reveals Tim. He had to adjust to not only his inability to walk but also to the changed attitudes of people around him. "I was sought after in social situations before the accident. Now I have to be aggressive and assertive. If I'm not assertive in social situations, I'm going to be left behind—all the time."

Mike lost his hair when he was twelve. "I got involved in a lot of fights. I decided I'm a regular ol' guy and I'm not gonna be the one laughed at sitting in the corner." The question persists, "Why? Why me?" For some it is just an accident—something that happened. For others, it is part of God's plan—yet unknown or perhaps being revealed.

Everyone wants to be accepted and respected for who they are, not for how they look. Whose responsibility is it? Many of the heroes and heroines in this book feel they must take on the weight of being accepted. Mildred, who counsels others with cosmetic problems, believes, "Until I give off vibes of strength and acceptance of self, I can't expect others to carry me." Judith has stuttered since the age of two and generously concedes, "I do present myself as a person not so terribly handicapped. And that really works wonders. You can't control it, but at least you can contribute to the best possible response on the other person. And people do need to be set at ease." That thought is repeated many times by others.

There is society's responsibility, too. "Take people for what they are, not for what labels they have on them," Ginger (deaf) urges. "This is me—take it or leave it," laughs Mike (alopecia). Bonnie, who has a weight problem, says, "Accept the person first as a person and let *them* work on the weight." As Browning so aptly wrote, "It is a stone thrown into a stream and the water must divide itself and accommodate itself, for it cannot remove the stone."

How can we break down the social and emotional barriers formed by visible differences? Honest and open discussion of the problem is one way. We found that within families and among friends and in the schools, often the differences were *never* mentioned. "There wasn't enough time." And yet when we approached people for interviews, they dropped appointments, came at our convenience, opened their homes, submitted to our tape recorders, and thanked us when we were finished. Why?

Studs Terkel, the master interviewer, wrote in his book *Working*, "The privacy of strangers is indeed trespassed upon. Yet my experience tells me that people with buried grievances and dreams unexpressed do want to let go. Let things out. Lance the boil, they say: there is too much pus. The hurts, though private, are, I trust, felt by others, too."

The people interviewed were asked questions relating to their childhood, schooling, social and work life, and religious beliefs. At the end of the interview they were asked for a message to society. A few simply said, "There is no problem," but most were ready with a profound statement that had been on their minds "a good long time." Let us listen and learn.

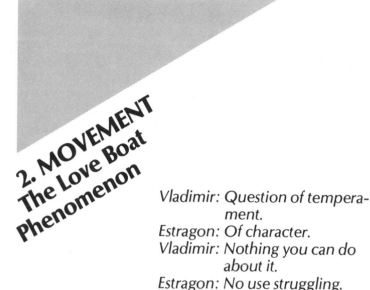

2. MOVEMENT
The Love Boat Phenomenon

Vladimir: Question of tempera-
 ment.
Estragon: Of character.
Vladimir: Nothing you can do
 about it.
Estragon: No use struggling.
Vladimir: One is what one is.
Estragon: No use wriggling.
Vladimir: The essential doesn't
 change.
 —Samuel Beckett in
 Waiting for Godot

MOVEMENT

Cerebral Palsy, Amputation, Lameness, Scoliosis, Muscular Dystrophy, Multiple Sclerosis, Spina Bifida, Polio

Barriers for the physically handicapped include stairs, curbs, narrow corridors, and escalators. Attempts are being made to remove those barriers. Once the handicapped have entered our buildings, social and emotional barriers caused by stereotyping, curiosity, and fear often prevent them from being fully accepted. The stares become worse than the stairs.

The mobile handicapped speak of two major social problems. One is *the stare*. "Everyone turns around and looks at me" (Mary, polio). "If they want to look at me, fine, but they don't have to look me up and down" (Paul, amputee). "Are you really that offended that you have to keep staring at me?" (Rich, scoliosis).

The other problem is *the concept of spread*. "They think my brain is in my knee" (David, cerebral palsy). "This guy has a disability so he must have every disability known to man" (Tim, lame). "I was put in the mentally retarded class for about a year" (Allan, cerebral palsy).

Knowledge is the surest cure for misunderstanding and curiosity. It is important to learn the correct terminology as well as to know the expectations and limitations of physical handicaps. Resolving the confusion will be a start toward removing the barriers and permitting the persons with visible physical handicaps to become our supervisors, co-workers, and friends.

TERMS:

Amputee: A person who has lost a limb or limbs due to accident, illness, or birth defect.

Cerebral Palsy: A condition which affects brain centers having to do with muscular control. Some cases are due to brain injury at childbirth; others are due to infections by the mother during the early fetal stages. The Rh factor may be implicated. There are symptoms such as *chorea* (involuntary jerking movements), *athetosis* (a slow writhing type of constant movement), poor sense of balance, tremor, and spastic muscles. Though there may be mild to severe impairment of intelligence, often a normal or superior intellect may be hidden behind difficulties in communication.

Lame: Able to walk, but with difficulty or with the use of crutches or a cane.

Multiple Sclerosis: A disease that attacks any part of the brain, spinal cord, and nerves with spots of degeneration; it is characterized clinically by paralysis, numbness, blindness, deafness, unsteady gait (ataxia), impairment of speech, and mental changes. It usually begins during the early years of life, most often between 20 and 30 years of age. There are periods of remission and relapse.

Muscular Dystrophy: An intrinsic disease of the muscles. The cause of muscular dystrophy is unknown; however, it often affects several members in a family and it seems that some abnormal chemistry is inherited which progressively destroys muscle tissue. It often makes its appearance in young children. As it progresses, it may incapacitate the patient so completely that he cannot even stand or sit. However, there are many forms of the disease, and not all lead to total incapacitation.

Polio (poliomyelitis): An acute viral disease characterized by inflammation of the nerve cells and resulting in a motor paralysis followed by muscular atrophy and often by permanent deformities.

Scoliosis: A lateral curvature of the spine. Idiopathic scoliosis begins in childhood or adolescence and gets progressively worse until growth ceases. The cause is unknown.

Spina bifida: A spinal malformation in which some of the vertebrae fail to fuse so that a sac containing the covers of the spinal cord, the fluid, and even the spinal cord itself may protrude between the split vertebrae and appear under the skin. It occurs at any spinal level but is most common in the lumbar and sacral regions where it is associated with severe neurological disturbances including paraplegia and loss of bladder and bowel control. The surgical treatment of spina bifida depends on the defect and degree of neural impairment.

CEREBRAL PALSY

PAT (A Volunteer)

Pat is living in a three-room apartment in a complex for the elderly and handicapped. She has gotten there after a long period of trials beginning at birth. She feels her accomplishments are remarkable considering the odds. Cerebral palsy causes her to walk awkwardly. Her right arm and hand are almost useless. Her speech is understandable but is slurred and her voice is high pitched.

I've always felt I had a story to tell. Everyone is flabbergasted that I've made it. I was born in Washington, D.C., as a twin. The next fact I know, I was adopted at three. My adoptive parents were looking for a playmate for their first adopted child. I don't know what the intricacies were, but I do know I didn't walk. They adopted me anyhow and they took me to doctors. I was diagnosed as having infantile paralysis. I have reason to believe they either couldn't accept the disability even though they adopted me or they thought I would get well and I didn't get well.

My adoptive mother was not well emotionally. One problem I knew she had was that she couldn't ride the bus because she thought people stared at her. So when she walked down the street with an uncoordinated, disabled child, she couldn't cope with it.

When I say she couldn't cope, I have to tell you how she coped. She squeezed my hand real hard to make me straighten up and walk right. I remember the squeezing and I remember sitting in the car because she didn't want to take me. My first feeling was that I was at fault and I was in the wrong. *Somehow it is normal for a child to feel if you just do better it won't be so bad.* Well, it never got better, it got worse.

I went to public school. School was a haven of rest because home was unbearable. Socially I was the only one in the school with a visible handicap. I was able to get through it somehow. I remember not being happy at all.

I was a slow writer so things were difficult. By sixth or seventh grade I'd go into history and they'd be talking about war, and I wouldn't know what war they were talking about. Things were a blur. I could have done better. We would all say that, wouldn't we? We were taught about A group, B group, C group, and even that little D group. Well, sometimes I was in C and D, and I always felt that if I could write or if I could pronounce, I would be in A. But who knows?

It's very common for children to pick on other children whether they're normal or not. The schoolchildren were pretty well controlled. I didn't feel included, but I remember turning jump rope. I couldn't jump. I wasn't allowed on seesaws. I wasn't allowed on swings. I wasn't allowed to run. My sisters teased me about a redhead, a boy in school whose hands were never clean. To be teased about the dirtiest boy is a put-down. I realized it was a big laugh, biggest joke if I liked a boy. So I remember deciding, well now, Pat, you can like someone, you just don't tell no one. Understand that most disabled persons are raised asexual.

Did you know that you had cerebral palsy?

I knew I had something. I knew I didn't walk right. I think I thought of myself in terms of what I could and couldn't do. I was made to button buttons and there's no such thing as can't. You just spend hours trying to button buttons even if the buttons were up here [pointing to her shoulder]. I knew there was something wrong, but I was the only one in that situation. My parents swore that I never tried. My father had cut his hand a long time ago and it was supposed to be numb, but he still used it. He thought if he could use the numb hand, I should be able to reach out and grab a glass and not have the tremor. Oh, I didn't even eat at the same table with them because of the way I ate. I ate with my back toward their table. I resent it now, but at the time, that's the way it was.

My father had convinced me that I didn't do anything right. I remember, in defiance, I guess, going out the kitchen door, singing, "Yeh, I know you're right. I don't walk right. I don't talk right. My books are a mess. My room looks a mess." I don't know whether that's an excuse, but being CP [cerebral palsy], it's hard to excel as a child.

I hate my voice. I was told all my life that I was whiny. Even when I wasn't crying, I was yelled at for whining. And I didn't know what to do.

What are you going to do when you grow up?

Well, the whole time I lived under a cloud: "What are you going to do when you grow up? We're not going to take care of you." I know now that I drew some conclusions about that statement and the conclusion I drew is that I would wind up— you know—a street woman. Because welfare was a no-no and the work ethic was strong.

You could list on your hands the careers open to women. I knew my hands weren't very good. At one time I wanted to be a nurse. My mother's reaction to that was, "Boy, you go to give someone a needle in the arm and you'll give it to them in the head." After I found out I couldn't get a job, I began to do housework. I found I couldn't get along with people. I was crying and angry and taking offense. I lost a couple of housekeeping jobs.

How did you feel about yourself?

I wanted to end it [life]. I couldn't make friends. I couldn't work. The whole work ethic. B.V.R. [Bureau of Vocational Rehabilitation] sent me to business school with another girl who had CP. We almost didn't get diplomas because we couldn't type. CP—being misunderstood—no one knew what to do with it. All disabled people knock rehab—like wow!

I seek out those who operate on my level. The intellect becomes the best thing you have. The physically disabled disdain those less intelligent. The Disabled in Action groups have less patience with anybody who doesn't keep up. They wait for people to fall on their face. The physically disabled are intellectual snobs. You know why? It's a basic thing. Disabled people probably feel bad that they are disabled. *Who feels good about being disabled?* When you feel bad about yourself, it is easy to put others down. It is not unique.

I get remarks like, "Oh, you are intelligent!" They're surprised. I sort of developed a way to speak so I come across the right way. But if you're with someone, they tend to ask the other person something they should ask you.

Reaganomics are causing me to go downhill emotionally. When we were getting programs, we were making progress, we were somebody. Now it is easy to feel with everything shut down, we are nobody. Who cares?

Last year I was asked to be on the task force of an advocacy group. This is a group of mature people—not a disabled group. I'm more comfortable with them. The president nominated me for vice-president. I was overwhelmed. I was high for a while. Well, vice-president, you know. It blew my mind.

If I could write better—that's what I would wish. People don't realize how valuable hands are. There's very few things you can help out with physically without the use of your hands. You can't make a casserole for friends when they're in a jam, you can't baby-sit. *Being slow is overwhelming.*

I just came back from a spiritual retreat. Someone there said God conceived us millions of years ago—that's a mind blower. If that's true and he knew I would be adopted and mistreated and have CP, that doesn't fit. You just can't think about it.

ALLAN
(An Information Referral Specialist)

Allan is a thirty-four-year-old man with the combined disabilities of athetoid cerebral palsy and a severe hearing impairment. Moderate athetoid cerebral palsy is a central nervous system condition. Allan's arms, hands, and head are frequently involved in involuntary movements, making many actions difficult and his speech hard to understand for the unfamiliar listener. This attracts curiosity and attention. The severe hearing impairment means that Allan must wear a body level hearing aid. Communication has been a major obstacle for him. He holds a technical position in a civil rights agency.

I remember the teacher asking why I couldn't hear, or why I couldn't listen harder. I remember times I wondered why my teacher was angry with me.

This was at the public school for "crippled children." That was the name of the school at that time. Now it's called Widner Memorial School. They couldn't seem to deal with a severe hearing impairment because nobody had hearing impairments at the school. The students' main disabilities were physical disabilities, including polio, CP [cerebral palsy], and spinal cord injuries. I was put in the mentally retarded class for about a year, because of the communication problem I had. When I proved that I was ahead of everyone, they put me back in the regular curriculum. When I was in fourth grade my homeroom teacher wanted to transfer me to the school for the deaf, but I needed the physical therapy and occupational therapy.

Occupational therapy—I remember it took me a while to tie my shoes because they were asking me to do it in a certain way and I couldn't do it. So I did it my way. I remember people, including the therapist, telling me I couldn't do it that way, but I couldn't seem to do it their way. So since that time I've been doing it my own way.

My high school counselor thought I was not college material because I had cerebral palsy. They knew I was smart, but they covered it up. When I was in eighth grade, I read the part of the textbook on mathematics that had to do with algebra. A problem came up with the principal and counselor. "Why do you want to know about algebra? You know you're not going to go any further." They gave me a whole battery of IQ tests, achievement tests, aptitude tests. They timed it very strictly. Because I was slow, I got an IQ of 76. Then I had a label on my head—moderately mentally retarded. I don't know if they did that to discourage me from going on to college, or if they did that for another reason.

So I learned algebra on the sly. My teacher and my father both were teaching me my mathematics, and in my other courses I was pretty much self-taught. The grammar book I did in two months that my class took for a whole year. I did the history book in about four months. I was finally permitted to take one academic course my sophomore year, an English course. I did very well. The next year I was permitted to take English and French.

Adolescence

Adolescence wasn't an easy time, that's for sure. I noticed my difference more than in the earlier years. I noticed it more because I had a hard time going out. I felt isolated from many of the people I went to school with. My friends lived in one part of the city and I lived in another. I had to rely on SEPTA [public transportation].

Many of my peers just watched TV programs. I couldn't relate to them because I could never follow the show. I had hobbies. I was interested in the countries of the world. I collected postcards from all over the world. I read newspaper day in and day out—that was *my* thing. Yet most of the conversation that went on in school was about TV. I didn't find others with similar interests to mine.

In my early teenage years, I noticed a difference between

me and my CP peers. I couldn't understand what they were saying most of the time. Communication becomes more important as you get older. The more I look back, the more I find communication to be my major impairment.

Of course, there were good times—similar to the *shet*, that's Yiddish. Remember the pogroms? Between the pogroms there were the good times, the *shet*. Like the times my family went to Atlantic City to the beach. And I remember my bar mitzvah. And I would go on trips with my classmates from school. These were the good times.

I went away from home to college at Gallaudet College for the Deaf in Washington, D.C. That was the first time I really felt accepted by my peers. I had to learn sign language when I got to Gallaudet, of course. Once I learned sign language, I became more and more accepted. I still wish I could sign better.

When I went to NYU to graduate school, my first roommate was from Japan. That was an experience in itself. It was his first time in America. He came to this country to learn English— and he gets a strange kind of guy with CP for a roommate. I had four ears, four eyes, and a head that was like a helicopter. He had a hard time with me at the beginning. I remember he wouldn't talk to me for about four weeks because he just couldn't fathom the whole thing. In Japan, until recently, they hid disabled people from public view. It was very much an education for him. Even when I was talking, he was like a blank wall. I would keep on talking. After the fourth week, he started coming out of his shell. I learned a few words of Japanese, he learned a few signs. Since that time, we've been really close. He's gone back to Japan, but we continue to keep in touch.

On the job

My disability is a challenge on the job. I need reasonable accommodations on the job. For example, I use a sign language interpreter. I use a teletypewriter instead of a telephone. I do my writing on the typewriter because who can read my handwriting? I can't read my own handwriting. My boss is really an unusual person. He's very sensitive to my needs. He does his best to help me on the job. A long time ago my co-workers accepted me. Now I'm considered one of the bunch; one of the crazy guys.

It's hard to get around

My disability can get in the way for me when I want to go somewhere and there's ice and snow on the ground. This morning I was afraid to walk on the ice. I just couldn't do it. I asked people to help me. Several people walked right by without even paying attention. Feels bad sometimes.

I always want to be able to try to do things for myself. But what I can't do on my own, I should be able to feel free to ask. There are many times I wish someone would help me on the ice. If people want to help me, I wish they would ask—not just do it.

I live in a rough neighborhood. In the day, it's okay, but at night—forget it! I'm young—you can't make me stay home. I was mugged once when I was walking home from the subway. They were nice muggers. I tried to fake a faint and they helped me on the way down. For a while, I didn't feel safe at all, even in the daytime, but I got over that. When you're on your own for a five- or ten-minute walk, what can you do?

I remember one time, not long ago, when I was walking past the subway, a group of young white people started to make fun of me because of the way I walk. They laughed at me. I do see that sometimes in the black community too, but not as much. There are all kinds of Jews, but I haven't had any cruel experiences from Jews.

I do receive some very strange reactions. Some fundamentally religious people approach me as if they want to heal me. Sometimes they touch me and ask if they can pray for me. It seems strange, but that's from a different culture. Sometimes these incidents happen in the strangest places—on the subway, in a supermarket, on the beach.

I met a few girls whom I liked. I lived in the international dorm where I met some women that I dated. Communication was the big problem. Then I met a deaf woman, but I decided not to pursue it because of problems with public transportation. I'm not keeping myself from marriage—just waiting to see.

Allan's message. I like people to be themselves. Ask me questions! That's why I'm always putting on a friendly front, so people will feel more comfortable asking me, once they are able to break the ice. It's not *verboten.* Many disabled people—not all, but many—want to feel free to be friendly with nondisabled people. When other people seem uncomfortable, I can help by joking.

I'm lucky in a way. I have to accept myself for what I am. My brother is not disabled, but we are similar. We're different, also. He has tended in the past to go after the very best, or forget it. I have tended to feel that "a half a loaf is better than nothing." I'm the mess who made it. I made it *because* of the disability. I made it to be the person who I am, because if I didn't have the disability, I probably wouldn't have had the challenge. A person has to know how to use his disability, how to make the best use of what they have.

I say, try not to be discouraged. It's easier said than done, I know. I've been through hundreds of times when I have been discouraged. But I find I become stronger after that period. The message for people is basically be your own self and be the best at what you are. Don't try to overdo it. *Accept yourself for what you are.* Be the best at what you can be. If you don't accept yourself, how can you expect society to accept you?

BERN (Unemployed)

Bern has cerebral palsy. He explains to children, "When I was born, some of the wires crossed in my brain and that means I cannot send messages to certain muscles, and this causes my strange walk."

I have cerebral palsy which affects my limbs. It's a motor disability. There are obviously things I can't do because I can't get up speed. My speech is not affected. My thinking is not affected. By and large, I live in a "straight" world. I've perhaps overadapted to my disability. I'm inclined to think it's not all that bad being disabled.

Many disabled people lack socialization and I consider that partly their own fault. Outside of a few little things, I can do anything I want to. I've had to keep that idea very firmly in mind. It works except that it cuts off my communication with disabled people. Like any overcompensation, it has its disadvantages—you lose something while you gain something.

The first inkling that I was different must have come when I was four, five, or six. I went to public school. I remember the first day at recess. There was a certain amount of hopscotch, which I couldn't do; a certain amount of in and out the window games which obviously I couldn't do. It seemed we skipped back to the schoolroom. I didn't skip back so the teacher had to pretend I was skipping. That made it pretty clear that I was not doing what the others were.

I was not aware of getting special treatment at school. Of course, I didn't play games at recess. I never quite dug up enough resources to fill recess with good activity. I was always happy to see recess over. My first-grade teacher was a distant relative, so I knew her before I went to school. She may have played a part in the insistence that I enter into normal life. At dinner one night I was using my knife and fork funny, and she said, "No reason why you can't hold a fork properly."

Articulating it was sort of a circular process. My mother was not telling me exactly and I was careful to go along with her understanding lest she be hurt by my hurt. So it took some time before we leveled with each other about it. My mother knew that I had overheard somebody talking about my disability and she was very angry at that person. I recall I said, "Oh, don't feel too bad. I've known it all along."

My parents had a nice combination of firmness and sympathy plus a willingness to level now and then. My father told me once or twice that he really was bent out of shape that I had CP. He had played baseball and stuff like that. He liked to go hunting and I could not share [that] with him. He would take me along and I would get tripped up by the underbrush.

I had good friends. I was always part of the gang when we got to the gang stage. Dating, I was left behind for a while. But I never felt absolutely *out* of it. I always went to games, sports events, and wrote some cheers and fight songs. But I tended to be president in, for instance, the lab society.

The nice thing about being disabled in a small community is everybody knows you and everybody's got over that a long time ago. Strangers in town would find me strange. And always CP people get mistaken for drunks. A new kid in town says, "What's the matter with you? You drunk or something?" And the town bully is inclined to be particularly threatening to disabled people. Assuming that the bully has problems, it's likely he will take out his problems on somebody who has problems.

I was a built-in wallflower

Being a teenager is very difficult for disabled kids. Dancing is a common denominator among teenagers. Unless you have a wheelchair and a wheelchair partner, you can hardly dance. I was a built-in wallflower. The whole sexual thing is put into strange perspective. Disabled people, knowing they are different, are gonna be very uneasy about sex anyway, and then if they don't have a context in which they can test it out, it's worse. Not driving is a big problem, too, 'cause an awful lot of teenage life is now around cars.

One of my good experiences in adolescence was attendance at a church camp. I thought of being a minister and then I decided against it. The basis of my decision against it was ridiculous, I realize now. It was the communion that worried me. I was worried about spilling stuff. That is quite ridiculous. Reflecting now, I think I could have done the pastoral stuff and the preaching. But I decided to be a teacher. There was a lot of feeling against disabled people as teachers forty years ago. But I fought through that because of a terrible shortage of male teachers at the time. I got a job, of all places, in a military school. I survived a year and went on to teach elsewhere. I didn't have a rapport with students who were primarily activity inclined. I had good rapport with kids who spent more of their time in their heads.

The only trouble with life—your fourscore and ten—is that you can't try everything. I don't know that I'm sorry I became a teacher. I've done a lot of things better than being a minister. It's just one of the roads that one would like to go back and explore. But then, you're not the same person you were back then.

I know my bag of tricks

I am not self-conscious because I know my bag of tricks is sufficient for practically any situation. When I was working on a magazine, I was meeting all kinds of people—interviewing college presidents, people from overseas. I never felt uneasy. I learned some tricks in debating to keep people listening to what I'm saying. I establish myself immediately—assuring people that I'm not in pain. I think the key is to short-circuit your own sense of uneasiness. If you push that away, you've taken the first step. If the disabled person feels uneasy, then actually the able-bodied person is going to feel more uneasy. The one thing you can control is your own sense of comfort.

I take the burden. I don't know if I should. I can be too jovial, too happy, too obviously not in pain. I come on. I have discussed this with a friend, a psychiatrist who is a counselor of disabled people. We discussed the idea that disabled people sometimes fall into the trap of clowning. I have known a number of disabled people who seem to clown unduly. It's a defense mechanism. It's a cover. Another form of overcompensation.

I can be just too bright in what I'm saying. That puts people off. They feel you're climbing on top of them. You have to observe other people and yourself and it takes a certain amount of introspection.

Difficult social situations are anything that involves standing. I'm always miserable at a party. I can only stay in one spot so long. So in order to communicate, I communicate very rapidly. There's a herky-jerkiness about it. I can go sit in a corner and let people talk to me, but that's stupid, too. I'm always uneasy in crowds anyway for fear of getting bumped or knocked over.

I have a tendency to get dependent

I did marry kind of late—into my twenties. I was careful to be sure I could make a living. My first marriage didn't work too well. I don't think it was my fault or the effect of my disability. My ex-wife was a very bright woman, a very talented woman; I blame it all to the social change. She was very much in the forefront of the women's movement. We have three children. I don't think my disability affected my relationship with my children unduly. I am not able to carry my kids around. They are kind of cerebral-type kids.

Carol [Bern's second wife] and I get along quite well. I am sure that I irritate her. I help with cooking but I complain about having to get down to the lower shelves of the refrigerator. I don't do my share around the house. I have a tendency to get dependent. It's very easy to become dependent in little ways.

Get the curiosity out of the way

I think the nondisabled could be a little bit more bold about discussing disabilities. It's a touchy topic but it doesn't have to be. Obviously people are curious. Get that curiosity out of the way. That helps get the uneasiness out of the way. A disabled person can handle this. You can't count on the other person to handle it. One of the good things about the last twenty years or ten years is that there's been an increase in understanding what disabilities are and an openness about disabilities.

I notice a good deal more understanding of disabled people on the part of the general public. The idea that they don't break is getting through. The idea that if they want help, they'll ask for it is getting through. People are learning that disabled people have interests and talents just like everybody else. They're not all one little lump of disability.

The reaction I get from strangers is pretty much what every other CP person gets. Quick, size this guy up as to whether he's a nut. We draw attention all the time. You get used to it and anticipate this reaction. People try to talk to Carol around me. I'm inclined to let that happen cause that usually happens with people I don't care to talk to anyway. I establish myself with waiters and waitresses. I do the ordering.

The person who feels constrained to help is reasonably sensitive about it. I don't mind somebody saying, "Hey, can I help you cross the street?" Often someone rushes up and says, "Hey, can I do this for you?" That doesn't bother me at all. Sometimes I say, "Yeah, that would be nice." Usually it's because I need the help. Sometimes I think, "Why should I bother explaining to this guy that I don't need his help?"

A very nice thing happened to me getting off an airplane not too long ago. I was very tired. It was at the end of a very strenuous weekend conference. I was puffing up the ramp and a person alongside of me said, "This is really terrible, isn't it? This huffing up the ramp is really too much." I knew that was a suggestion that he was ready to help me if I needed help. I thought that was a very adroit way of offering help. I said, "Yeh, sure is." So we kind of leaned on each other. It gave me a perfect opening to ask for help. It was identifying with me and the problem, sharing the problem.

Kids are often quite frank. They say, "What's wrong with him, mom?" The mother says, "Look, I told you we are not going to talk to strangers. Come look in the window. There's a very interesting toy over there." Mothers shut the kids up by shaking them. I think a mother can get around it. "Sir, would you explain why you are limping?" I would just head right into it. There's no point in teaching the kids to avoid differences. Anything that gets around that is going to speed social change. I'd rather see parents head into it and make a mess of it.

Bern's message. Identification with all types of differences is much to be desired. These silly categories are very cruel. Obviously they are the product of ignorance. People accepting themselves and accepting others seem to go hand in hand.

It's obvious that Americans identify up. I've been working with unemployed people and they all have this Horatio Alger thing. If I work real hard I will never be unemployed and very soon I will be the president of the corporation. This blinds them to the fact that they may not and blinds them to the fact that others are unemployed. Identifying down is maybe too much to ask—asking people to identify with the poor and powerless.

The first step is to identify with your peers and we don't do that terribly well. The community is the basic unit of life. Individualism is no longer appropriate in the U.S. Hold your individuality within the community but don't stand out from the community in isolation or fear.

All those prejudices I could do without. Not only did society's stumbling blocks deprive me, but let's be grand about it—it deprived society.

DAVID (A Minister)

David has been a friend of ours for nine years. His limp doesn't prevent him from playing a wicked game of volleyball. He is thirty years old, newly married, and is a Church of God minister.

At first I could not walk at all. I had to have an operation when I was three and a half. I hadn't been able to walk at all until then. My earliest recollections were of having to do exercises and of wearing braces. I guess I was five, six, and seven years old. The doctors taught my mother some of the basic exercises that I had to do over those first years.

I had another operation when I was ten. My feet were turned inward and the operation was to straighten that out. A second operation was to try to straighten out the back of my knee, but it didn't make any difference. Two or three years ago I was working as a chaplain in a community college in Indiana. When the doctor saw me there, he took an interest in me. He talked to another doctor and they had me come in to just check me out to see if they could do an operation. They were just curious. I did take an exam, but the doctor said, "If we operate on you, there's really no guarantee that there will be any change. It really wouldn't be worth your time." So I just left it there. But I was curious because it had been so many years. I thought, "Maybe there's been something new."

I went to a regular school. One time after we'd moved, I was placed in a special class in New York, around fourth or fifth grade. It was an upsetting experience for me because they were very slow mentally—real problem students. But before the end of the term was up, they put me into the regular stream. I was bothered that they'd put me in there in the first place. It really bothered me.

I feel I had to earn my teachers' respect. But once I would prove myself, they would kind of forget that there was any disability. Depending on the temperament of the child, the teacher has to spend some time either to bring him out or, if it is aggressive behavior, to see where the anger is—to see where the bitterness is that could affect the child's relationship with the group.

My parents worked hard in trying to make me feel that there was no disability, that the biggest disability would be the barriers I put on myself. They always encouraged me to do my best. I didn't talk too much with them about it. My dad was very busy for one thing, and I never felt it was a problem big enough to talk about. I just did a lot of trying to deal with it on my own.

Adolescence was a tough time

I was very shy with girls [during adolescence]. I would get along well with them, but not in the realm of boyfriend-girlfriend. That was tough. I would wonder if it was a matter of the disability or some other things. I always struggled with that. Those kinds of things I didn't share too much with people. I had a few close friends that I would talk things over, but not too many. The problems I had at that age I don't think were so much in terms of my disability, but of who I was and where I was going.

My best time was between nineteen and twenty-two. That was a really good time. The college life. I had some very close friends. I was able to develop more independence. I made a serious commitment to my faith which also made that a rewarding time.

Perhaps my sensitivity to other people was heightened because of my disability. I can't imagine how I would have been without it because I've never had the chance to see. I think it did heighten my sensitivity to others and also made me aware of who people really are instead of just taking one look and saying, "That person is this way or that way." I tend to have more compassion and patience, too.

I still have to deal with people judging me on outward appearance. I always have to overcome that before I can enter into a good working relationship with someone. I just realize that's the way people are. I have found that as I establish a relationship, people tend to respect me for who I really am.

If I had faith

In a situation as a pastor, I always have to contend with those who believe I should be healed or, if I had faith, I'd be healed from my disease. I say to them that my inward character determines my behavior. I tend to say to them not to be so quick to determine what God wants out of one person's life. I haven't thrown out the idea that it could happen to me—a healing could take place, but I'm not striving to see it happen. I'm not living for the day. If it's going to happen, it's going to happen.

Sometimes I did question why God created me this way. The peace I got was reconciling the fact that God *did* create me and he created me as he would. It wasn't mine to question how he created me, but it was mine to use what he had given me—my talents, my gifts—to his glory. And I strive to do that. God planted people in my life who helped me to see and value myself for who I really was, and that was a tremendous help for me, a tremendous help. People would say, "We don't even see your disability anymore, because we see you." I began to see that my own feelings were probably larger than the perception of others, so I dealt with it.

I have wondered what it would be like to not have my disability, but I'm not sure I would like all the implications or the changes it would bring about because I *do* like who I am. I don't think it would make any difference now, because I've reached a point of maturity.

David's message. We put people outside of society because of some assumptions we make when, indeed, they can be not only a part of society, but a very rewarding part of society's growth. There is a vast resource of untapped abilities in the handicapped that society should have the tools to encourage.

AMPUTEE

PAUL (A Supervisor)

Paul is a good-looking, well-built young man in his early thirties, engaged to be married. He is missing an arm due to cancer when he was 22. Paul works as a supervisor in a family owned business.

It started when I was in high school. I had a tumor in my stomach area that was nonmalignant. Two years later when I was in college, I had another tumor up in my shoulder area. It was malignant and it spread and resulted in having to get my arm removed. That was ten years ago. I didn't go back to college. By the time I was feeling good, I had gotten involved in the business and I didn't get a chance to go back.

They didn't give me any counseling in the hospital. I didn't need it. I was young. I had just turned 21. I didn't need any counseling.

I have three brothers and they really helped a lot. They stuck by me. They helped me out. I never really talked to anybody about my problems. I'm a very quiet person and keep everything to myself. I'm independent. I always like to do things myself. Maybe that's why I can do things now the way I am because I just have to do things myself. You just have to be a strong person and make yourself do it with a strong mind.

I'm not involved in going to any handicapped groups. I just

want to be healthy. I don't want to hear other people's problems. I just want to be with normal people. Maybe it's good to be with people like that, but you just segregate yourself.

I am a supervisor in the business. I like to work around machines. I like to work with my hand. I like to work around tools.

Do you consider this a handicap in your work?

[Hesitates] At times it is a handicap, but I just bear it and I don't think about it. At times I have to get somebody to do something for me. The people I work with all know me and they help me right away. Everybody's aware of it. They know what I can do and what I can't do. There are things I could do if I had two arms that I have to ask other people to do—that's frustrating. But I can do just about anything that anybody else can do.

Don't look me up and down

I know people are going to look at me but I don't pay any attention to it. I used to look at people. Now, being handicapped, they look at me. I sometimes feel uncomfortable with a bunch of strangers because I know they're going to look at me. When they keep looking at you, that bothers me. I just like people to accept me as any normal human being. If they want to look at me, fine, but they don't have to look me up and down. Some people have enough nerve to ask me what happened. I don't know why people do that.

Definitely the younger children are more curious, but I understand that. They ask questions. Between ten and thirteen, they're asking questions.

Why me? you know. You get answers in the long run. I'm getting a wife. It's hard to say if I would have met the same girl. There's a big difference between me and my girlfriend. I'm ten years older than her. I've been around. I've known a lot more people. I didn't settle down until I was about 25. I'm surprised I'm getting married now. I'm the last one.

PAUL'S FIANCÉE, DENISE

Paul's fiancée walked in and I asked her about her initial reaction to Paul

His loss of an arm didn't bother me at all, even at first, because he has such a great personality I completely overlooked it. I never even thought about it. If a person is missing a limb, it doesn't erase the whole person and what he is. That's one place where I think people make mistakes. They think if a person is crippled or in a wheelchair he or she is worthless. Me, I think that is the wrong way of looking at it. And I never looked at that in that way at all.

How did your parents react to Paul?

They asked me what happened to him. They said, "You're unbelievable. How can you go out with somebody like that?" I said, "What's wrong with that? Just because a person doesn't have an arm, or doesn't have a leg, it doesn't make any difference. You don't know what he's like. You don't know him like I do," and that's just the way I answered them. And if they thought that was wrong, fine.

People don't understand you just have to accept things like that. If they looked at it the right way, they would be able to see that it doesn't make any difference. The person is a person.

Getting married—did it enter into your decision?

I love him and I didn't even think about it. The only thing that bothers me is when somebody says something to him, I'll go back and I'll say something to that person. I get mad. He won't do anything. I'm the one. I'll say, "What are you looking at? Watch it." I get mad because I love him. It annoys me when people continue to look at him. And if they say something. I'll say something. To protect him. I don't know what it is. Overprotection. They turn red or they walk away. They feel guilty. Then I like it. I think, "Good. I made them feel bad." 'Cause I don't think it's right. Sometimes I'll say, "What if that was you?" And then there's silence. People that think they're *it*. People that think they're better than others.

God's plan—I think there's a reason for everything, and God makes things happen so other people can realize how lucky they are. It makes people act better and realize what life's really about.

Paul's message. I accept it. I get along fine.

Maybe if people would really take a look at people who are handicapped and give them a hand when they see they are having problems. . . .

I know how it feels to be in that situation. You appreciate it when someone helps you. I was in a store one day and I didn't even know this guy and he saw that I was having a problem and he said, "Here, let me help you." I didn't even know this guy. It's always nice to see somebody give you a hand. It doesn't happen very often. I appreciate it. I do. I feel bad, but I appreciate it. You just go and say, "Let me give you a hand."

If you see someone having trouble in a wheelchair, help; if you see a blind person, don't just stand there and look. If you see someone having a problem, help.

LAME

TIM
(A Vocational Rehabilitation Counselor)

Tim is an intake counselor in a rehabilitation center. Now in his twenties, he became lame in his teens as a result of an automobile accident. He walks with the aid of lastrum crutches. Tim had been a runner and had been thinking of trying out for the Olympics before his accident.

I was involved in an automobile accident a little over eight years ago and sustained a head injury. I was in a coma for a month in pretty bad shape, then in and out of a coma for another month, and in another hospital for physical therapy for another two months. I was in a wheelchair at home for the rest of the year—going every day for outpatient therapy. Then regular crutches for another year. I've been on lastrum crutches for possibly six years.

I think I knew the prognosis on some level, but I wouldn't admit it. I needed time. It was a gradual process. I don't have recollection of any tremendous depression. It was more of an evolution. I think that adjustment to disability is a very evolutionary process.

My family reacted very well although they were actually very distraught and very upset. I've come to the realization that one of the most important things is how significant-others react, especially to an acquired disability. When I started to recover, my family gave me enough room to test limits, at the same time offering me the protection that was there in the family situation. When I went away to get my master's degree, and when I moved up here, my mother said, "We hate to see you go so far from home, but after all, this is what we hoped and prayed that you'd still be able to do.

Now I have to be agressive and assertive

I was very much more reserved before I was injured and a lot more withdrawn, especially in social situations. A lot less self-confident. Before I was injured, I was a very good athlete. I had been very active. I was really just starting to think about trying for the Olympics in '76. I planned to run. I was also a basket-ball player. To a big extent, I didn't have to have confidence in myself. I was sought after in social situations. Now I have to be aggressive and assertive—very self-confident. Because if I'm not confident in my own abilities, no one can have confidence in me. *If I'm not assertive in social situations, I'm going to be left behind—all the time.*

I don't have any hesitation or reservation about inviting somebody on a date. I don't think every rejection I receive in life is based on my disability, or I'd go crazy. For a while, I slipped into that, but wonderful as I am, there are some people who just don't want to know me, just don't want to do things with me. There are so many things, so many hassles in life I have to deal with anyway, I just can't worry about why some-one doesn't want to date me.

It's the concept of spread

If I hadn't been hurt, I wouldn't have been a rehabilitation counselor. I was interested in politics. Now I think that politics is a point to get to down the road. I hope I'm heading for the same end. I'm just taking a different road to get there. Eventually I want to get into politics, but right now this is what I want to do. If I wasn't disabled, I wouldn't be doing this right now. I think there will be certain hurdles to overcome to get into politics. I find that would be true with most things. *For everybody there are hurdles to be overcome; for the disabled there are more of them.*

For me the biggest hurdle is probably attitudinal—not my attitude, but other peoples' attitudes. That's the one thing in my relocation process that I wasn't prepared for. I was involved in psychiatric, psychological contacts that were all concerned with my change. "Okay kid, are you going to be able to handle it?"

Instead I was deluged with the fact that I had to handle all these changed reactions *to me.* My opinion was thought so much less of when I came back to the world as a handicapped person. Some of my associations had significantly dwindled because, you know, "We don't want to talk to this guy. What does he know? He's a handicapped person." It's probably the result of not even listening to what I have to say. To some extent, it's the concept of spread. This guy has a disability, so he must have every disability known to man.

People disassociate themselves a lot less now. I can only assume it's because I'm becoming more comfortable with my own disability. I almost force them to associate sometimes. Because I'm a wonderful person, you know, and I almost knock them down. I can't afford to be standoffish about anything.

My master's degree was on the discrimination of the visibly physically handicapped. I found it to be sort of a catharsis for me. I could put down some of my experiences. Putting them on paper released my feelings. The handicapped as a group are taught to deny it. Kind of be bigger than life. You know, "This doesn't bother me. This isn't a handicap." People will come up to me and ask me about my condition. "You ever gonna get better?" I say, "No." They say, "Oh, you'll get better, I just know." I don't know where they know it from.

Most of the TV programs and the movies are starting to come around now. In the past they always showed a person with a disability overcoming it, and going on to achieve fantastic accomplishments. I term that the "Love Boat Phenomena" where everything in the end works out.

Everything is beautiful. Everybody goes off in little pairs, hand in hand, and everything is great. And life isn't like that, you know. This is real life. *If you can't get a clear view of what's going on, how are you going to deal with it?*

Tim discussed an effort he was involved in at college to secure parking spaces for handicapped students

I used to run down to school even when I didn't want to do anything, just to create a hassle. Just to say, "I'm handicapped, and I'm going to demand my rights!" I think it's great if I'm visible instead of feeling it's bad if I'm visible.

I've been to restaurants many times when the waitress or waiter will say to the people I'm with, "What will he have?" When I'm with a person who knows how to deal with it, they say, or I'll say, "Why don't you ask 'he'?" I like that. I say the important question is, "What is 'he' going to tip you?"

I'm never uncomfortable just because someone else is uncomfortable. I never buy into guilt. I think guilt is the most useless emotion ever invented.

God must have some wonderful plan for your life

I converted to Catholicism about four years ago. I grew up in the Southern Baptist Church. After I was injured, some people in the church started rushing up—leaders, real leaders in the church, would rush up to me and say, "Tim, God let you live through this terrible thing. He must have a wonderful plan for your life. Some great plan." I was eighteen years old, and not only did that put pressure on this newly disabled person to do something great in his life, but if you really think about that, in my way of thinking anyway, if God let me live through this terrible thing, he must have let the terrible thing happen. I couldn't deal with believing that God had anything to do with what happened. The accident was a freakish accident. A trailer came loose from an oncoming car and there was nothing I could do. I think that God just provides strength to get through this life.

My family was close before, but it brought them closer and made me more assertive. If I didn't have a disability, I wouldn't have to be more assertive. The only thing that upsets me is running, my athletic endeavors. Not the fact that I can't do it any more as much as that I think I was good. I know that I had a shot at the Olympics and even doing well in the Olympics. I know that I would have tried as hard as I could and given it my best effort. But I'll never know now. I'll go through my life and never know.

It's made me more sensitive, more caring, more sympathetic. I think I'm more mature. It's widened my experiences, made me more assertive, given me more self-confidence.

Was it worth it?

No. I had to go through a lot of pain and suffering to get here.

Tim's message. I would say that people should ask if they feel they want to help me. If I don't need help, I'll say, "No, thank you. I can do it myself. Thanks for asking me." If I need help, it's appreciated. Talk to me about the accident if you want to. I would ask if I was curious about something in your life, within limits.

You have to provide for the handicapped the things that will enable them to function within society. You have to have parking spots for people with mobility difficulties. You have to have interpreters for those who have hearing impairments. You have to have this and you have to have that. To deny that and say we're just going to make it equal, is not equal. These people can't do something or they wouldn't be called handicapped.

SCOLIOSIS

RICK
(An Office Worker)

At the time Rick's parents noticed his curvature of the spine, their doctor told them to wait until the end of the summer for treatment. Rick feels that if he had been treated immediately, his present condition would not be as severe.

It's called scoliosis which means curvature of the spine. What people are afraid to say is "hunchback." The only experience little kids have had is the infamous story of *The Hunchback of Notre Dame.* It's the only word they know. Some people try to say "curvature," but most people are at a loss.

Doctors say you can be born with it; you can have it all your life and not know you have it. The severity of mine is what makes it apparent to the public. There's no reason why people are born with it. They don't know if it's hereditary or not. My father had injured something or other near his back and he was x-rayed. He found out at the age of 55 he had slight curvature of the spine. But for 55 years he was not aware of it. There is an argument for it being hereditary, but then other people get it with no trace in their background.

The Milwaukee brace

One of the options I had when I was 13 years old was to have the spine opened up and set straight. It would take a recuperative period of about eighteen months where I would be flat on my back and unable to move in a cast. It seemed very, very frightening and it seemed terribly expensive. They did have an alternative which is the Milwaukee brace. Why "Milwaukee," I don't know. You'll see teenagers with their chins propped up in a brace and it looks like it's stretching their necks. What people don't see is that it goes all the way down to their waist and it pushes and pulls on the tension bar to actually stretch the spine because the tissue for some reason is soft. They have to wear it until they reach maturity, meaning bone-structure-wise, and it's different for boys and girls. I think for boys it stops at 21. It can develop in very small children and they wear it until they are 21.

I wore the brace for two-and-a-half years. During that time they kept taking X rays every three months to see if my spine changed at all. It didn't improve it, but it didn't let it get any worse either. They assumed after that time that it wouldn't get any worse and that's why I stopped wearing the brace.

My most difficult years were the years I was wearing the Milwaukee brace because I had the most stares and stood out. Kids didn't mention it. They didn't talk about it. But if they were to bump into me, they had an overreaction of, "Excuse me, I'm sorry. Did I hurt you?" I usually hurt *them* because the steel brace made me invincible, but they thought I was fragile. I was a man of steel, in the literal sense.

When I was wearing the brace, people sometimes asked me how I was. It was superficial. It is compared to asking people at work, "How are you today?" And if you start to really tell them, they think, "I didn't want to hear this. I just wanted you to say, 'Fine, thanks.' " I thought they were trying to come across as concerned, but I felt they were asking because they thought they were supposed to. When I would take the brace off, they thought I had done something good. I had accomplished something, and they congratulated me. But when I had to put it back on, it embarrassed them. It is compared to someone who had a disabling disease, overcame it, and then had a relapse.

I wouldn't have wanted my teachers to explain to the class

what was wrong with me—at least not while I was present. But I wouldn't mind if many different problems were explained and this just happened to be one of them. If you take a collective range of things that could be wrong with a person and why certain disorders happen, or what certain conditions look like— syndromes or whatever can happen to normal people through no fault of their own—that would be a good way of educating the public.

The stare

It would be almost impossible to create a mass sense of people not staring at a person because they're peculiar. If you did that, you'd have people not staring at women because they're good looking. There are times when people stare much more intently than others. There's a stare that there is no ill intention. Then there's a stare that makes me think, "This is it. Are you really that offended that you have to keep staring at me?" I had a co-worker several years back who would stare. I found it very annoying because he had seen it day after day after day for many, many months. It was particularly rude that he still stared at me.

You can get tied up in it too much. People may have been staring into space and then they realize they're staring at a deformity, go into shock, and apologize because they don't want you to think they were standing there staring at you for the wrong reason.

It's not a big thing, but I've almost entirely stopped going to the shore, to a crowded beach without a shirt, or going swimming in a swimming pool or anywhere I would have to be without a shirt or clothes. I guess part of it is in my head. Certainly a T-shirt doesn't hide everything. But there's something about being stared at and having no clothes on the area that stands out that intensifies embarrassment. I miss being able to swim. It's probably something I could overcome if I felt it was a real deprivation, but it's a kind of deprivation that I have caused myself, not that anybody else has.

I can thumb my nose

A few years ago I discovered that I was pretty good at skiing. Not water skiing, of course [laughs], but snow skiing. You bundle up with jackets and equipment that are colorful. I feel good on skis, and its equated with a sport that I was denied because of awkwardness in my youth. I discovered all of a sudden this sport that seems very much admired comes easy to me. I'm having a great deal of fun, and I feel, in some ways, superior in the fact that here's some big guys that are brawny and well built and tall and attractive who get on skis and they're absolutely helpless. It came so natural to me that I feel a false sense of superiority. That's probably the only area where I can thumb my nose at the other things that have gone by.

I'm so close to being normal

I am sure there was a stage when I cried and thought, "Why can't I be normal?" I have one of those things that I'm so close to being normal and so close to being terribly deformed—being right in the middle. I can go for a whole day without thinking about it and then suddenly it becomes very apparent. It's not like blindness that every second of the day you're conscious of being blind. It's something that comes into the consciousness and then goes out. It's out more than it's in.

I'm not particularly religious, but I used to think, "Maybe I'm being sent this particular bad thing and that's gonna be on one side of the seesaw and a lot of good things are going to happen to balance it off." I've always had good health. I usually miss one day of work a year, and that record has stood since the day I started working. I don't think that way now, though. I just don't think there is any particular reason I was picked to be the way I am. It may help make me a little more sympathetic to a person with a similar condition.

Rick's message. It pays to know a little bit more about what causes deformities. Try to teach yourself not to be embarrassed by them or turn away or stare too long. Years and years ago when our parents were younger, they remembered a generation when it seemed that everybody had some kind of deformity. You'd notice people with a limp or people with a mole or people that had a short arm or only three fingers. Because there were so many people around, nobody noticed them much. Now we're in an age when surgery can correct a lot of things early on. It's a wonderful thing—but surgery's never going to be able to put back a limb that isn't there or be there at the right time for everybody, so there's always going to be some people that stand out. We have to get used to the idea that not everybody fits into the mold of perfect health.

MUSCULAR DYSTROPHY

SUZANNE
(Unemployed)

Suzanne is a young woman who has been in a wheelchair since she was in the fourth grade. She is a beautiful, intelligent, outgoing person and feels her experience in a special school for "crippled children" was isolating.

When I was born, they really didn't have any idea there was anything wrong with me. It wasn't until I started walking that there was any indication of anything. Certain symptoms. Like the way I walked upstairs. So when I was five, they did a muscle biopsy and diagnosed me as having muscular dystrophy. I went to regular public school for kindergarten and first grade. By second grade I was walking on my toes. They put me in the hospital to lengthen my heel cords. I was cast both legs to the hips. They didn't hold me back in school; in fact, they were skipping kids from second to fourth grade that year and they skipped me, too. For fourth grade I was still casted so I had a home schoolteacher sent by the public school system. That was around the time it became increasingly difficult for me to walk. So when time for fifth grade came, they enrolled me in Widner [school for "crippled children"].

I *always* knew something was wrong with me. When I was about three or four, I couldn't do a lot of things because I would get tired. I could walk, but I couldn't run and I couldn't jump rope. I was a great "steady-ender." It was just one of these things that you just accept. I used to fall a lot and there were two of the girls who were real good at getting me back on my feet. They'd always included me in things and they wouldn't tease me. There was a boy or two that did, but the girls always stuck by me.

I completely lost the ability to walk by about eighth grade. I could transfer myself, that sort of thing. But by about ninth grade, I couldn't do that either. And that's when I sort of leveled off. I guess it was a quick process by any other standards, but to me it wasn't like week to week I could tell I was getting worse. I really couldn't tell.

The hardest part was early on, around eleven and twelve, because my friends were a little bit older. They were really into the boy-girl thing. There were lots of parties and music. I was sort of semi-invited to the parties, but I wasn't really included. The boys never really considered me one of the possibilities. I would come home and I would just cry. I remember very vividly that feeling of being there, but not being there—not being included. They would tell jokes and I didn't know what they meant, but I laughed along with them. I learned to play the guitar around that time. I was in demand for that. I think that was a big help in getting accepted.

My best years were when I was very, very young, around age five, and my later college years—both of them because I was very secure, at ease in my surroundings.

You gotta mainstream them from kindergarten

I think my friends knew there was something organically wrong with me. There were some things I couldn't do, but they would come to me when they needed help with their math homework. We did plays and musicals and that was always *my* department. These kids were not special in any way, they weren't brilliant. That's my whole thing about mainstreaming. You can't mainstream kids from eighth grade on. You gotta mainstream them from kindergarten.

Socially, you've got to get people out into the mainstream as soon as you can. It's like teaching kids a language. It's so difficult to learn a language after you hit a certain age. You get the normal exposed to the ones with disabilities and then they're not afraid of people with disabilities anymore. I think there's gonna be a sort of natural closing in of the ranks. When there's need, the other kids will help. I really believe that.

I was not mainstreamed because my neighborhood school had too many steps. So I went to Widner. I went there for sixth grade through high school graduation.

Don't have grandiose goals for yourself

When I went for an interview at Widner, I remember sitting there outside the office because they didn't have a waiting room and all these kids were going by me for lunch. I'd never seen kids with disabilities before, and all of a sudden they're throwing me into this situation with all these disabilities.

I would never, knowing what I know now, have a child of my own go there, unless they had certain types of disabilities where they need physical therapy and the sort of thing that the school offered. I didn't get any of that stuff. It wasn't indicated at the time. *I think it was just too much of an isolating experience.* Lots of kids were much more isolated than I was because when they went home, they had no friends from home. I started out with friends and experience. I think it gives you a false sense of yourself and you pay attention to your disability when you really shouldn't, and you don't pay attention when you should. It's sort of like screwing up your values and it's really not a realistic outlook on the world. The kids would joke around about their disabilities, but they never really discussed them and how it affected them. They never really got to the basics of how things were going to be when they graduated.

I turned sixteen two weeks before college. In a way, it was better I graduated so young, because I was out of that stifling atmosphere I had been in. So I actually grew up in college. It was hard, but it was better because I had a lot of people around, a lot of experiences that I *never* would have had in high school. I met with *all kinds* of people instead of that close-knit group. I hated having those same friends for all those years in high school. And especially since I didn't particularly like them. I was forced to be good friends with them. I had nothing in common with these people except that they were disabled.

When I went to Widner, I got A's and A's and A's, and a B here and there, without really working because the standards were so low. I did not apply myself because I didn't need to.

I know they were coddling the students. They were saying things like, "It's a big bad world out there and you should be glad for what you have now. This is a great school. You're getting a great education. Don't question it. Don't have grandiose goals for yourself."

There was one teacher that was hated by most of the students and she was hated by me for a year or two. She pushed her kids. She saw the ones she thought could get some place, and she hounded us. She made me work really hard, and I would say she's the only teacher who really helped me out in any substantial way.

I went away to college and all of a sudden. . . . I mean, it's difficult for *anyone.* If you're at the top of your class, you're not gonna be at the top when you get to college. I was pulling C's and I was working and it was very difficult for me. There were times when I was ready to just pack it all up and leave, but there was nothing for me to go to, so I stayed. I must say that was the only reason why I stayed. I'm glad because after about six months to a year, everything was fine. I finished and I did well. I never got all A's in college, but, who knows, maybe I could have if I had developed better study habits.

I decided to change, and I changed

I did a lot of crying when I went to college. A lot of feeling very, very scared and lonely. It happens to everyone who's a freshman and goes away to school. It doesn't happen overnight, but all of a sudden you realize you're in a group of people having lunch together every day, and then you're meeting friends and going out to a party. You realize you're in a group of people and they're all your friends and . . . you're not lonely anymore. So it happens—but you want it to happen right away because you're so scared.

I actually had to physically force myself to be outgoing. My sister, when she was twelve or thirteen, came along when my parents took me to college. She was the last one to say goodbye; and in her infinite wisdom, she said to me, "If anybody invites you to go someplace, no matter what, go!" It seemed like such a little thing. I'm surprised I even remember it. But a couple days after that, some people invited me to go get ice cream and I didn't want to go. And it was a big hassle— who was going to get me in and out of the car? And I really didn't feel like eating ice cream, anyway. But I went. After that, I started forcing myself. After a while, I didn't have to force myself anymore. I decided to change and I changed. You can change what goes on out there, if you just force yourself to.

On being questioned if she feels a child should be encouraged to use crutches instead of relying on a wheelchair:
There was a time when I had a physical therapist come in after the casts were removed in fourth grade, and he did as much as he could with me. He stopped because there really wasn't anything that could stop the progression of the dystrophy itself. I guess being in the wheelchair was sort of a relief because it was so difficult for me to get around otherwise.

It's good to use crutches in some ways because I think it makes the child not give up. But I couldn't get very far. I would just get *too* tired. I could walk from one end of the room to the other and that was about it. And the wheelchair gave me a whole bunch of freedom to go and do things that I couldn't normally do on my own. In fact I had a motorized chair, too. I got it when I graduated from high school. There was a group of ladies from a synagogue who wanted to give a motorized chair to some Jewish girl. The principal thought of me. As the only Jewish girl there [laughs], it was a pretty easy choice.

I sort of fought this chair because I thought it was going to be making myself a slave to this machine. I was really afraid of it. I didn't want to try it out, but when I went away to college, I was forced to use it. I couldn't have people pushing me back and forth to class. It only took me a week or so, then I was never without it. I used it all the time. Not only could I go places, but I could go by myself. People do react differently to someone that's in a wheelchair than to someone that's on crutches. I think they interpret crutches as temporary and a wheelchair as permanent. It's really an individual kind of thing. I know people in wheelchairs that are just powerhouses and they get a lot done and they seem to really do well within their framework. And I know people in wheelchairs that are so disabled—not necessarily physically, but socially. It's just an attitude.

I know myself, I go out of my way to be outgoing. In a lot of instances, I'll joke about the chair. I'll make wheelchair jokes early on because that usually puts people more at ease. I mean, we can do Polish jokes and Jewish jokes and not really offend someone who's Polish, and I think you should just try to do some wheelchair jokes—try to desensitize the rest of the world.

All the time I see people turn their eyes and try not to stare. As soon as I smile, they get real embarrassed. I sort of enjoy that once in a while. I don't blame them. If I see somebody in a wheelchair, I look. Then there's the people that are obnoxious about it. The ones that will really look at you as if you are just a piece of meat.

There will always be buildings that are not accessible
When I first went to college, one of the departments was not accessible. If someone wanted to be premed, they could not do it. I was doing certain library work where I couldn't reach the shelves, but I solved that. I had a close friend that would go to the library with me anyway. I decided to make him work for me. I would pay him and he would help me do my research. He just really did the legwork and I did all the brainwork, you could say.

It is very unfair. I applied to Princeton when I was getting ready to go to graduate school and they told me they could not accommodate me. *That* I think was unfair. I may not have qualified academically, but I wanted a stab at it. But they didn't even bother to go through the academic pathways.

After I graduated from graduate school, I went to live with my relatives in Miami. I lived with them for a year and I taught in the Miami schools. I loved it, but the funding ended and so did my job. One of the major reasons why I decided to leave was because I really couldn't live with my relatives forever. I needed to find myself a place to live in an independent living situation—and I couldn't. I worked at it really hard. I put up posters in different places and registered with a roommate finder service and put an ad in the *Miami Herald*. I could not find somebody that I could trust enough to live with me. I can't transfer myself and I need some help dressing. I need someone that's reliable for my most basic needs and I just could not find someone to live with me. So my mom said, "C'mon home."

I was unemployed for a year. I had interviews for all kinds of jobs—personnel, social service agencies. Sometimes my transportation was too expensive to afford to take the job. There was a van service I could use, but they charged an arm and a leg. A trip out to a rehab center the other day cost $35. You couldn't do that every day.

The Septa [public transportation] buses with lifts are a waste of money because they are totally under-utilized. The philosophy is good, but in practice it is a *total* waste of money. I can use them, but my motorized chair won't fit on them. The drivers are obnoxious. They don't really want to take the extra time. I've never seen anyone else use them but myself. And they don't go everywhere; they only go in certain areas. You have to be able to get to the bus stop to use the bus. The para-transit* takes you from door to door. It's exactly what they needed in the first place.

---

*A door-to-door public transportation system covering certain parts of the city

The disabled *can* travel. There are places for us to go, but you need to give more attention to detail. It just takes more time and energy, and that's all it is.

My mom and I decided to go to Disney World when I was graduating from college—just to take a little vacation. She went to the travel agent in the neighborhood and made reservations. Disney World is very accessible. She found us a great hotel, accessible, "right across the street from Disney World." (If you know anything about Orlando, *nothing* is across the street from Disney World.) So they said, "No problem. There's a shuttle from the hotel to Disney World." It's a bus—with steps! It worked out because people are nice, and I'm small, and there's always men around. So they lifted me off. But what if I were a 200-pound man?

There was an opening at Penn for this one job. It sounded really good, working for the assistant to the president. It involved all kinds of great things, like writing and editing and liaison between department heads. It turns out the president's office is in an inaccessible building. They have money to build an elevator, but that didn't help me. That really hurt a lot because I was really qualified for the job. Now there's no excuse for the president's office to be inaccessible to those handicapped students. That's the first time it's really slapped me in the face like that.

What advice would you have for prospective employers of the handicapped?

Just ask questions early on. Don't wait and get all these crazy ideas in your head that the person may need all kinds of adaptations. If you just ask them, nine times out of ten the person will know what needs to be done, if anything. It just may mean moving two desks apart. To me, honesty is the best policy. You run a risk 'cause there may be some disabled person that's militant about their disability. They insist that everything be accommodated to them. For me, if it means going in the

side door and not having a ramp in the front, I'll go in the side door. *Just to be there.* I always try to mention that I have muscular dystrophy because that's really the one question they want to ask most: "What's wrong with you and will you get worse?"

If an employer had a disabled person on the job that wasn't working out, he should tell that person as he would any other employee. Just because we're disabled doesn't mean that we're really any more special than anyone else.

Does government have a role helping handicapped out with extra financial burdens?

That's one of the conflicts I've had for many years. Just because I was disabled, I was getting SSI. At that time I don't think I had extra expenses. I didn't have any outstanding medical bills. And I always felt that was wrong, except that I saved a lot of that money. One of these days I'm gonna need that money. My biggest fear is to have to be in a custodial kind of situation. I pray to God I never have to do that. When I move out, it will not be to a place like that. It will be on my own. So I guess if it were between help from the government and going into one of those kinds of places, I would definitely accept it. Ever since Widner, I've always wanted to get away from the disabled. I wanted to be out there with the real people, all kinds of people.

Little eye glances

I've always found people to be extra courteous. I do appreciate it. Usually if I get close enough to a door, I don't even have to ask because people will come running. Every so often we'll go somewhere where there'll be a step or two. People in the hospitality profession will come over and they'll take me up themselves. That happens a lot. I like it. I really do. I much prefer to like the people that I'm patronizing.

And I see the kids who say, "Mommy! Look at her!" and, "Shut up, Junior." It happens a lot in restaurants and department stores. The kid'll look up and say, "What's wrong with you?" Usually I'll answer him. Then you see the people as they're walking by, give you one of these little eye glances so they think you don't see, but I always do. I always look at them and they get embarrassed. I've never had anyone [be] really rude. Every once in a while people's toes get run over [by the wheelchair] and everyone always has the same reaction. They turn around and look at me and say, "Are you all right?" like I'm attached to the chair. Sometimes I'll say, "Of course, are you okay?" And they always say, "Yes." Meantime, they're limping away.

I think that people are insensitive by ignorance. Because you have one disability, they think you have more than one. They'll speak louder; they'll talk to me as though I'm retarded. People have asked my mom questions they should ask me. When I go out to eat with someone, they always give the other person the check, and usually I'm the one paying.

I'm really limited socially

Now I'm really limited because somebody my age doesn't meet people in the street. You either meet people through your work or you go to school. I'm not really big on parties with tons of people I don't know. It's hard enough to meet new people, but I'm constantly faced with a new person meeting me as a person in a wheelchair. I like things that are centered on music. I like theater. But, you see, the one thing about these types of things is that they're not really social because you sit there and you watch what's in front of you. Going out to dinner is fun, also. But I'm so sick of eating. That's all we do in this country. We go to places where we can eat.

Guys?

Well, that's sort of a bust, I'd say, in my life. I've had lots of male friends. I've found it very easy to relate to men, so I usually hold on to them as friends, sometimes even longer than girls. I'm not real sure why that is, except that I'm smart and I think guys enjoy having girlfriends that are smart. They want to go out with the dumb ones, but they like to be friends with the smart ones. It's difficult to meet prospective boyfriends. I've had a few. When I was at Miami, I had one for about a half year at least. It was a really good experience. What I enjoyed most about him was he accepted me and then forgot about the wheelchair. We went places, which was unusual for me. You've got to get me in the car and get the chair in the car, go to the place, and get the chair out. For most people, it's a hassle to go somewhere with me. And he was very good about that. It's like he never even thought about it. I really appreciated that period of time because I got to do a lot of really normal things. We went to the beach. We went shopping. We didn't go to the opera; we didn't do anything cultural; we never went to the library. But I had a great deal of fun.

I really enjoyed that, but since then there has been no one and that's really a big regret I have. But I really don't know how to change it. I hate to say it, but I've just accepted it.

I don't see being married. I see more just a relationship with somebody. I don't think I'd want to saddle the responsibility of me on somebody's shoulders like that. It's almost like if I would love them enough, I would give them up, which is a really terrible thing to say. It sounds like I really don't have any value in myself. But I do. I think it would be sort of a drain after awhile. I would feel like they were staying with me because I needed them more than they needed me. Maybe if the situation did arise, I would feel differently.

I don't blame anybody

I just assumed that it was one of those things that you get. I asked a new doctor I had for my dystrophy and he said as far as they know it is hereditary. We can't trace it back to anyone. But there's a defective gene that's carried in 1 in 10,000 people, and if two people marry that have that defective gene, one in every four children they have will have dystrophy. I just think of it as a freak thing that my mother and father got married. It's just chance. I don't blame anybody. Not my mother—it's not like she knew ahead of time. I really didn't know for years that I had dystrophy. My parents never told me. I do blame them for that. I wish they had told me.

There are many different types of dystrophy. The one that everyone knows about is the kind that's contracted by boys. They just get progressively worse and then they die before they reach, say, 21.

When I was about 14, I watched my first dystrophy telethon. When I saw this telethon, they were saying, "Give money because these kids will die." They weren't saying there were other dystrophys. Here I was fourteen. I thought, "I've had two seven years, and I have one more to go." I was so upset. There was always that question in the back of my mind for many years after that. And even around the time I hit 21, I was thinking, "Well, I'm still going strong. I don't think I'm going to kick off." Finally I got re-diagnosed and they told me that it seems I've leveled off. I'll probably get hit in the rear end by a truck and that's how I'll die.

I never spoke with my parents about it. We just never talked about it, which is strange. But, see, it didn't affect our lives. We made the adjustments and then we just lived.

Suzanne's message. We need to make people stop making snap judgments. Try not to judge people. Accept people as being innocent until proven guilty. Instead, every time you see a black person, don't think they are a thief; or every time you see someone in a wheelchair, don't think they're retarded. Try harder to think of people as individuals. It's very easy to generalize and we all do it. How can we change that? I don't know that it's possible. People, even though they don't like to be generalized, like to be part of a group ... they sort of like to be generalized.

I'd like society to know that people with physical disabilities are just like everyone else. Everyone is just an accident away from being disabled.

There are plenty of disabled people that are special, intelligent, creative, and musical. There are plenty of disabled people that are wasted, of low intelligence, and not motivated. It's just so important for people to realize that underneath those disabilities, there's the same person.

MULTIPLE SCLEROSIS

AL (Unemployed)

It wasn't until I asked Al for an interview for his alopecia [see page 116] that I discovered he also has multiple sclerosis. Al is able to walk but often needs the assistance of a cane or crutches. He is resisting using a wheelchair. Al is married, has two teenagers, and was active in camping, scuba diving, and rock climbing until the multiple sclerosis curtailed his activities. He talks about the adjustment he and his wife have had to make to his "new self."

They don't know what causes MS. There's a lot of veterans coming back from Vietnam who have it and they think it might have something to do with Agent Orange. There's some people that think it's a virus. MS has been around a long time. It seems to be regional. You're more likely to find somebody with MS living in the Middle North Atlantic region than in California. They've not been able to attribute it to any one special type of person. It starts anywhere between seventeen and maybe twenty-five years of age. Being in my early thirties, the timing was right. If I look back on all of the things that might very well have been the result of MS, it could very well have gone back to the time when I was sixteen or seventeen years old.

I think back over a number of years in my life and I can now point out episodes that, had medicine known a little bit more about MS, they probably could have discovered it back even as far as high school. I had a disease known as reticloma neuritis which is inflammation of the eye. Now that is a dead giveaway that MS is imminent. There is nothing they can do about MS. You learn to cope is what you do. If I had known that I had it, I don't think it would have made a lot of difference.

I was always strange as a kid. I never bothered with a doctor until whatever I had affected my mobility. When I got to the point where I couldn't deal with it, then it was time to look for help. I had gone out to California at the end of 1978 to my nephew's bar mitzvah. I had lost quite a bit of weight. I dropped close to sixty pounds in less than a month, which ought to be a fairly good indication that perhaps something isn't right. That's when the tremors started. Body tremors—arms, legs constantly shaking—so bad that I couldn't hold a cup of coffee with one hand. I was having a little bit of trouble with my eyes and my voice would slur on occasion. It just got to the point where we decided that maybe somebody ought to look at me. I went to my regular doctor and he couldn't put his finger on it. We have a friend who's a neurologist. I went to him and he took a look at my eyes and did some tests; but, as is the case with a lot of doctors, he doesn't like to deal with friends. He suggested that I contact Dr. Silverberg who is with the neurology department at the University of Pennsylvania. I called the doctor and we made an appointment for Tuesday, and I was in the hospital by Thursday. It was the end of November.

I was in from the end of November until the first of the year. Christmas and New Year's is a wonderful time to spend in the hospital. They give you time off for good behavior. They let me go home for a one-day break. At that time they thought it was sarcoidosis. It's basically a neurological disease and it affects the brain and spinal column. That's how they found it to begin with—after the spinal tap. Along with a lot of other strange and exotic things they do like a CAT scan, ultra sound myleograms, ENG's, EKG's, and all sorts of weird things. The results were off enough that there wasn't anything they could put their finger on. It wasn't this, it wasn't that. MS is not something that is just diagnosed—it's usually the last thing after trying to rule out everything else. It affects different people in different ways. I'm fortunate, I guess, that it doesn't affect the upper body anymore. There's no more tremors.

Right now there's no cure. You go through periods of remission where the disease becomes minor or it can get worse. There are some people, I understand, that after dying at a very old age were found to have MS through autopsies and never knew they had it. There are some people who have one bad period and then it goes into remission and never comes back. I've gotten better in some things. The upper body involvement is completely gone. My eyes are fine, but I'm having problems with my legs. I can't walk. I'm wearing braces.

How did you feel when you found out you have MS?

I'm not the right one to ask that. I've always been unable to deal with not being in control. Angry is probably the first thing. I'm not sure at who; it was a nondirected anger.

There is at certain times a feeling of paranoia. I'm constantly looking over my shoulder to see if people are watching me. There was a period of time when I was under medication that it had quite an effect on me and my dealing with other people. I'm starting to come back around so the kids aren't afraid that I'm going to bite them. My wife isn't afraid that I'm going to snap at her.

I miss the things that I can't do now that I could before. I enjoy scuba diving. I like rock climbing. I like camping. I like walking in the woods. I can't walk now for any more than a city block without help.

I hate wheelchairs

I have rails on the steps and a banister going up to the second floor. Thank God my arms are good so when my legs aren't, I can get there. But the days that it gets so bad that I can't, I'll use the chair lift. I hate wheelchairs. The whole concept of the wheelchair is frightening to me. It's the stigma involved. They're big and they're bulky and they're ugly. By the same token, I looked at an Omega wheelchair the other day. It's called the friendly wheelchair. It looks like a motor scooter. There's just so many things that I want to do and if this little Omega will give me some of the mobility that I had before, then it's dumb not to use it. I mean, I owe myself to be happy.

Red alert!

The whole idea of having to depend on other people to do things takes longer for me to get used to. I do things even though I know I shouldn't until I hurt myself. I break things. I started using a cane because I couldn't stand up without it. Part of the attitude of me says, "Get help." The other part of me says that I don't want to have to depend on other people. You can't have both. You have to be willing to ask for help. One of the problems my wife and I are having now is a defense mechanism on my part. You reach a level of frustration and it's easy to snap out because you're not getting what you want. I've had periods where my legs will start to bounce and I can't control it. Rather than saying, "Hey, I'm having trouble with my legs," I'll flare and I'll snap at somebody. Right now my biggest problem is control. I find myself immediately going through a red alert without going through a yellow alert first to be able to let everybody know that I'm liable to snap at them. It's getting better than it was before.

Disease is hard on the person who has it, but I think it's harder on the person who is the spouse or the support person. You learn to live together, and then everything changes. You develop the rapport that you have. My wife and I were at a point where we almost didn't have to talk to each other 'cause we knew what the other was going to say or do. That's not there anymore. 'Cause *I* don't know what I'm going to say. I'm not as comfortable with myself now and I have to relearn myself and she's gotta relearn me.

We talk about it frequently—with the kids, too. It's funny; we explained the whole disease to them and we thought that we explained it fairly well. I guess the obvious question the kids have, "Is it contagious? Is it hereditary? Are you going to die from it?" The typical questions kids have. My kids are twelve and fifteen. Children listen at different levels at different times and they hear you but they don't listen to you.

We go to a support group every Thursday night—the Philadelphia MS support group. We had a session last week for kids. The kids started talking to each other in a group. They put the kids together and the spouses together and the patients together. Coming home in the car, my oldest daughter said, "But you never told me that you wouldn't die from it." I started to say, "Well, yes I did," but obviously she wasn't ready to hear that. They talked all the way home. I guess the time had come that they started listening.

I was sort of macho

When my gait got worse, I kept pushing. I continued to work. I put everything into the job. Looking back on it, I think my boss was very nice. I eventually ended up leaving the company at the beginning of October 1981 by mutual consent. I think they carried me for a while. I did my job. I got up in the morning. I worked my twelve hours a day or more. Came home and ate and drank myself to sleep. It could have been the medicine. It could have been the disease. It could've been a lot of things. I could've been feeling sorry for myself. I worked and I kept going. The doctor suggested that I not work but I guess I was sort of macho.

Finally, I physically couldn't work any longer. That was my last job. I am now at liberty. I am physically limited, although there are a lot of things I can do to get me back into the mainstream. A wheelchair is one of them. Hand controls on a car if it ever gets to be that bad. I'm thinking of selling equipment for handicapped people. Seems only fitting, you know. I thought it was a little strange that the guy who came in to show me the wheelchair walked in with it, as opposed to somebody who might have had to ride in it. Maybe I could offer something to people other than the piece of equipment. I would love to do it. I've got to do something. I can't sit around the house all day long. You can only watch so much TV and read so many books.

I am more aware now of the problems of people who are handicapped trying to get around. I was just in court in New Jersey because I got a ticket for parking in a handicapped zone in a mall. I have the tendency of being Don Quixote—chasing windmills. I refused to pay the fine. I ended up going there and I had to go in a wheelchair because my braces weren't working. I said, "By the way, I am handicapped. I certainly hope you have ramps down there and will be prepared to handle me when I come to court." The court clerk said, "Well, wait a minute." She came back and said, "We'll be ready for you." I'm not quite sure what that meant. Even with ramps, it was virtually impossible to get from one part of the place to another. The bathroom was down two flights. With a regular wheelchair, without somebody with me, I wouldn't have been able to come back up the ramp.

That's one thing that bothers you—all the lip service. On the other hand I was walking down the street the other day and I had a problem getting off the curb. When you have a cane and your legs aren't very steady, you have to stop and think about what you're going to do and which leg should go first. I actually had two people walk up behind me and offer me an arm. I appreciated that. I'm not sure that I'm bold enough that I would've asked for help. But that's part of the independence thing that I'm not quite used to. I probably would've fallen off the curb rather than asked for help.

When do you ask for help?

That's one of the things we were talking about at the support group last night. That's one of the areas where all of us have a problem. When do you ask for help? When do you say you can do it yourself? One of the hardest things about the disease is learning how to cope with it and learning how to deal with support people. It's difficult for them as well as difficult for us.

I'll tell you what happened. My daughter doesn't normally like to bring people over to the house because of my condition. She's embarrassed. This is the fifteen-year-old. I'm not upset with her. I can understand her problem. We had just come back from a support group meeting and I had decided that if she wasn't going to tell her friends and was not able to tell them without being embarrassed, that I would have to break the ice. When she had one of her friends over, I met her at the door. She looked at the cane, and I just said to her, "I'm sorry if I startled you, but I have MS." And she said, "Well, that's all right. My dad is on artificial legs." It blew my daughter's mind. The easiest way is to take the initiative and put peoples' minds at ease.

Al's message. There's room for all of us and it takes a little bit of understanding on the part of the people who don't have a disability to understand people that do. We don't have to beat down the doors to take a handicapped person to lunch, but just understand that we need to do the things that we like to do and try to make it easier.

There's lots of things that you'd like to see other people do, but that doesn't mean you can cause it to happen. You just have to decide what it is that you want to do and then just go about getting it done.

SPINA BIFIDA

BOB (Unemployed)

Bob has spina bifida which is a deformity of the base of the spine resulting from a failure of junction of the parts. From the point where the spine is open, Bob has no control over the lower part of his body. His legs and feet have not grown proportionately to the rest of his body. He is in a wheelchair. Bob lives at home and tries his hand at writing.

It's called spina bifida and sometimes it's called "open spine." I am actually missing vertebrae. That means I cannot walk the same way that you or anybody else can. If I did walk, I would need braces and crutches—which I did have. The last pair of braces I had were not right. They just did not seem to fit right. My dad took the legs part off and right now I have the back brace on. It's supposed to keep me sitting straight and also to keep my back straight. They've tried two spinal fusion operations, both of which have failed.

I noticed I was different when I was about five or six. Like most kids that age, I couldn't comprehend what was going on. "Why can't I do this, that, and everything else?" I was just wondering, "Why?" wishing that I could.

Did your parents ever talk to you about it?
[Long pause] No, the subject never really came up. I went to a school for handicapped children. It was run by the Easter Seal Society. I was six when I started. I didn't start to have

therapy until I started school. They had me going up and down stairs working with my legs and arms. That was about an hour a couple times a week. What was the result? It sure gave me strong arms.

We had social studies, English, all the regular subjects. I liked school up to a point. Seven years ago I left. Some people would call it dropping out. I call it just leaving, because I had a variety of reasons why I left. The main reason was I felt that they'd taken me as far as they could take me. I thought the time was right to move on and do something else. I did not graduate. If I had stayed there another three years, I would've. You had the option to stay there until you were 21.

I think it would have been better if I had been with ambulatory children.

Once you're put in an environment that's handicapped, it's like you're in a rut and you can't get out of it.

And if you do get out of it, it takes a long time. Thinking back on it, I guess it would have been better if I had gone to regular school.

Adolescence?

I wish I could have done a lot more at that time. That's about the time when you start thinking about driving a car and getting a license, which I have neither of. For a while I thought maybe it was because of my eyes. When I cover up my good eye, everything is blurred, but I can see very well out of the good side. But I don't think it was because of my eyes at all. I think it was because of this [indicates his body].

To drive . . . [wistfully]. It was about eight or nine years ago, a friend of mine with the same problem, was driving an equipped car. Mom busted the balloon like you wouldn't believe. "No! If Gary wants to kill himself, that's his problem." He got a license. He got his father's car equipped. He goes all over the place—driving his car. Gary and I come from two different worlds. Anything he wants, he gets and I think that's why he's gotten a car.

I go on errands every day

I'm not employed at all. I'm here at home . . . all the time, doing my hobbies. As far as employment goes, I'm not sure what I want to do. I'm trying to become a writer which is one of my hobbies. I have tried on a couple of occasions to see if I can sell something, but it didn't work out as well as I'd anticipated. But I'm going to keep trying. I do have my errands. I go on errands every day. I go and pick up the newspaper every day. Sometimes I will go out for lunch.

I get a lot of stares. Small children will stare. If their mothers and fathers are with them, sometimes they'll pull them away, "C'mon, let's go." If I need any help with steps or opening a door, people will do that. Some of the adults—which really bugs me—instead of looking at you and talking to you as a real person, they'll kind of look down at you and pat you on the head. It drives me aaggh! I dislike it!

I can get into the post office. It has a ramp on one side and steps on the other. That was my idea. I had to have someone mail a letter for me, so what I did—I was on a real barrier kick—I wrote a letter to the postmaster general in Washington and explained the situation. Exactly one month later, the assistant postmaster general wrote back to me, "We have assessed the situation and there is no possible way that we can arrange a ramp." And I thought, "Ha! Sure!" I made an appointment to see Congressman Edgar and I told him about how it was very difficult to get in places without ramps that had steps, including our own post office. To make a long story short, after I talked to him they put that ramp in the post office.

I don't date. I have made several attempts to get myself a, quote, "girlfriend," but have not been successful. These have been girls that I have known from when I went to school. It would be a sister of a friend I was going to school with. But it just wasn't meant to be. I don't think I'm going to get married. The reason is obvious. Look at me. I'm not saying I wouldn't want to. *I want it all!* Like maybe a kid or two. Just looking at me, I know it's not possible.

Why me?

I believe in God, very much so. Many times I thought, "Why me?" I wish I hadn't been born this way. My parents were both in their forties. I think if they had been just a little bit younger.... When there's nobody at home, I would say it out loud, "Why me?" God's got something planned. I don't know what it is, but it's something.

Bob's message to parents of a disabled child. Don't be too protective. That's the worst thing you can do. Let them find out what they can do. If they feel they can drive a car, let them find out for a while, see what it's like. Then if he or she can do it, good. If they can't, that's all right, too. Just let 'em try it. See if they can do just about anything, because they themselves know their limitations. They know what they can do. They know what they can't do.

To society. Treat the handicapped as you treat your own. We're human beings just like everybody else. We dream, we have feelings just like everybody else. We can think just like everybody else. All that we ask is that we be treated just like anybody else.

POLIO

MARY (Retired)

Mary, now in her seventies, had polio at the age of five which left her with a useless left arm and a twisted hand. A finger which has begun to turn upwards is causing her distress as she feels it makes her disability more noticeable.

I had polio. I was the only case in Lansdowne. So how do you get it? Nobody knows. I was five so I don't really remember it. They took me to New York to a specialist. They wrapped it in cotton which was the worst thing they could do to an arm with polio. You're supposed to exercise it. They thought then you were supposed to keep it still. So that's why my hand goes this way instead of the way it *should* go because it started out that way. This arm is smaller than the other arm, thinner, and shorter. And now for some unknown reason this finger started to bend up. *Everyone turns around and looks at me.* I can't lift things with that arm. I can hold on to things, but haven't any strength in it. Kids didn't tease me when I was a kid. They all knew what polio was. I couldn't use my arm in school. It just hung there at my side. I noticed a picture the other day of all the kids at Lansdowne Friends School where I went and you can just see my arm is hanging down.

I'm more conscious of it now than ever before. I used to walk up and down the block. One time I met a young kid—I don't know who he was—and he just turned around and looked at my arm. I thought, "I'm not going down that street again." I haven't told the doctor because I'm supposed to take a half hour walk morning and afternoon. So I've been doing it on the front porch. It shouldn't be enough to bother me, but it just is.

I don't mind if people know I had polio. It doesn't bother me at all; in fact, I think it's better if they do know 'cause then they're not liable to turn around and look. When I am walking my hand is like this [she shields her hand with the other]. I try very hard to keep my finger down so it doesn't show quite so much. I think some people notice. I have no doubt. It bothers me. They're just interested and want to know what happened, I suppose. They never *ask* anything about it. "What's the matter with you?" or anything like that. Sometimes I feel like turning around and saying, "I had polio. Go home" [laughs].

When I was a young adult, I worked for doctors. I loved it. I was a secretary-receptionist. My arm didn't seem to bother me much when I was in the office. I even wore short sleeves. Several patients came to me and said, "Don't ever leave us. We love ya," and stuff like that, and that made me feel good. I am that kind of person. I enjoyed meeting people and talking with them and being with them. My arm didn't bother me. I wished I could give shots. I always wanted to give shots. I can't put this hand up to hold the person's arm. I never gave shots, but the doctor didn't seem to mind.

And before we knew it, we were falling in love

Mother said to me one time, "How're we going to get so you can meet more people?" I said, "I don't know. I think I'll join one of these, what do you call 'em, 'men groups' that send out letters to girls and that sort of thing. I'll be very careful how I do it. If a man wants to meet me, let him come over here to the house." She said, "All right." I nearly dropped dead because I didn't think she'd agree to it. But she found out that I wasn't going out with anybody and she'd thought it was kinda too bad. I was fifty years old. And so, by gum, I got this letter from this man who said he was down in a hospital in Chester and he would like to meet me. It was a very nice letter. It wasn't "I love . . ." or that sort of stuff at all. He came up one afternoon and we talked *all* afternoon. And before we knew it, we were just falling in love with each other. We finally got married. He had heart trouble. I knew that he wouldn't live too long. We were only married four years. My arm didn't bother him at all. He took me places, took me to all sorts of things.

What now?

I'm more of a religious person now than I used to be because I'm all *alone*. I say my prayers. I have been thinking, "What now?" I try to keep my finger down when I go to sleep but I don't think it will do any good. It bothers me, just the sight of it when I'm walking along. It looks like something's wrong. It's silly, I know, because people probably just walk past and don't think anything about it. Nobody ever said a word [laughs] so I shouldn't worry about things like that.

Mary's message. I think if people don't look at me, I'm all right. I mean, sometimes I get so mad at a person on the street turning and looking, I feel like turning around and saying, "Yes, I've had polio."

3. COSMETIC
Hear That, Everyone!

Beauties in vain their pretty eyes
may roll;
Charms strike the sight, but
merit wins the soul.
          —Pope

How many goodly creatures are
there here!
How beauteous mankind is! O
brave new world,
that has such people in't.
          —Shakespeare

In war men need courage once.
Hers is every day.
          —Rebecca's mother

"The closer the handicap is to
where the nonhandicapped
person must focus his attention,
the more likely it is that the
interaction will be abbreviated."
          —Tim Coty, master's
thesis on Visible Differences

COSMETIC

*Birthmarks, Keloids,
Alopecia, Albinism*

When a birthmark covers part of the face, it often involves swelling of the eye, lip, or nose. The cause of birthmarks is unknown, but the effect is clear: stares, questions, remarks. It is particularly difficult during the teen years when adolescents "want more than anything to look like everyone else" (Rebecca's mother). Society must break through the standards of cosmetic perfection set by advertisers and set its own standards of acceptance and respect for individuals.

Generally it is not thought that cosmetic problems are handicapping. However, those with acne, facial keloids, and albinism tell stories of discrimination and difficulty in finding appropriate jobs.

The person with alopecia (hairlessness) is a natural target for jokes, but the two men I interviewed were ready for them. "I love the jokin' and messin' around," laughs Mike. "I'll make jokes about it," says Al.

People with cosmetic problems, more than any other group I interviewed, stress that they must carry the burden of responsibility for acceptance. "Keep yourself high," says Rebecca. "Act like you're really popular." Mildred declares. "Until I give off vibes of strength and acceptance of self, how can I expect others to accept me?" And they all emphasize that when people get to know them, the difference is soon forgotten.

TERMS:

Albinism: A hereditary absence of pigment from the skin, hair, and eyes. Other conditions such as astigmatism and photo phobia (extreme sensitivity to light) frequently occur. A slightly pinkish color in the skin or eyes is due to the blood vessels beneath.

Alopecia: Loss of hair. The cause for loss of hair in childhood is unknown.

Birthmarks: The result of enlargement of blood vessels in the skin or of some extra pigment in the skin usually occurring during the development of the baby before birth. Various types occur: *hemangiomas*—dark red type, often raised; *nevi* (moles) are brown; *port-wine stains* are flat and vary from pink to purple.

Keloids: Growths that appear in scars. The tendency to have keloids is inherited. They may sometimes be removed by treatment.

BIRTHMARKS

KENNETH (A Store Detective)

Kenneth works as a store detective in a supermarket. He has a port-wine birthmark on the left side of his face. He's a young married man in his twenties.

The port-wine stain

I was at Delaware County Hospital on Monday night because I had a cyst next to my nose. There was a plastic surgeon there and he took a look at my birthmark. He called it a port-wine stain. He invited me to his office and said, "We can now remove them with argon laser. Argon laser is the opposite of the red laser." The red laser they use to cut or separate. The argon laser coagulates blood vessels—the birthmark is enlarged blood vessels on the top surface of the skin. It's only good for the people who have the port-wine birthmark. On Wednesday, I went over and he showed me before-and-after pictures. He said, "I'd like to do a test square on you. After several weeks the crust will dry up and the scab will fall off and it will turn red like new skin. The new skin will fade into the rest of the color of your skin." I will go back in seven weeks. If it works, they do one square inch every three months. They allow time for it to heal. They say the success rate is 70 percent, but he's had 90 percent.

I've known about the laser since 1976, but it was just in the planning stages. In 1978 they were still experimenting with it. He showed me pictures of some guy who had some scarring from it, but they were doing it too intensely. They were trying to do it all at one time. On a scale of 1 to 10, they were using 7.0. When he used it on me the other day, he had it up to 1.5. So it's a lower intensity over a gradual period. He's had 90 percent success.

It's a port-wine birthmark. They know what it is—it's a number of blood vessels. They don't know what causes it. It does appear in the first few weeks of pregnancy. The only thing my mother can think of was she may have fallen when she was eight months pregnant. The doctor said no. It happens in the first few weeks of pregnancy. They don't know how it happens. There are all kinds of old wives' tales.

One woman, whose daughter has a birthmark, spilled wine from the table on her leg when she was pregnant with her daughter. When it spilled on her leg, she brushed it away. When the baby was born, she had a birthmark on her leg—the same spot where the wine had spilled. That's so far-fetched. Another girl that I know said she was born with her hand on her face. The doctor said that didn't cause the birthmark.

Kids are cruel

I had no problems before kindergarten. I didn't want to go to kindergarten because I knew that I was different. I dreaded going the first day. It was awful. I wouldn't leave my mother. I was screaming and crying. I remember that very well. After that I loved kindergarten. I had a great time. The kids didn't treat me any different. It really started about first and second grade. Kids are cruel, the old saying goes. When they actually knew that I had something different than they did, they made fun and called names—"purple people eater," and other names. I cried. I used to really cry.

Thirteen and fourteen years old were my fighting years. Kids got crueler as I got older. We moved to a different neighborhood. I used to get beat up a lot. They would pick a fight because I had a birthmark. I would more or less keep to myself. I was an introvert. It wasn't until five years ago, I came out of that shell. I stayed mostly to myself. Then somebody would make a remark about it, I would come back with a fist. That was all through grade school. It was mostly older kids that I had fights with—kids who were in eighth grade when I was in sixth. They had their own little group. I couldn't be a member of it because I was different.

I had a few friends. Usually kids who, you could say, were the outcasts. We had our own little group. John was part Spanish. They looked down upon him because he was part Spanish. Dennis was the class clown. He was from a poor home. His clothes weren't nice. They looked down on him for that.

I never dated in grade school. I had girlfriends, but I didn't date. I was never invited to a party. I always held that against them. I was never invited to a party. I didn't get angry at any one thing or one person. Just angry that I had it. I used to say a lot, "Why can't I be like everybody else?" My mother would say, "God gave it to you because you're special, you're different." It would comfort me then, but it wouldn't last.

When I got into high school, I decided, "I'm not going to be the gopher. I am going to stand up for myself." It was actually then that I started coming out of that shell. I was in my freshman year of high school when I met Caroline. She was going into eighth grade. Eight years we went together before we were married.

I still have that feeling there is someone looking at me. People are really ignorant. When I go to church on Sunday, I go in the back of the church. We park right at the front of the church, but I make excuses to go in the back. Caroline goes in the front. We just meet in church.

When we go out and eat in a restaurant, if everyone is facing me, I will switch seats. I don't feel comfortable sitting there eating. Not that I want to turn around and catch people watching me or looking at me or staring. I just feel uncomfortable that they might.

I can be walking down an aisle in the store and be looking

straight ahead. Someone comes walking up the aisle. I can see their eyes quickly turn, trying to get a peek. If I'm in the aisle, I'll look at something on the shelf while they're passing just so they may not get a look. I'll see children going down the aisle. All of a sudden, I'll see them in the next aisle. They want to get another look. It bothers me.

A lot of people are polite and a lot of people are ignorant. Polite: "Do you mind me asking what happened to your eye? Is that a birthmark?" Ignorant: "Did somebody punch you in the eye? That must have been an awful fight." I'd rather they'd just take a look and ask me politely than make a joke out of it.

A lot of people say they don't even notice it. My friends, they could care less now. But they're happy to hear about the treatment I'll be getting, and they're interested. One of the men I work with asked, "How did it go? Tell me all about it." We went through the whole thing. He was interested and happy something was being done. My aunt cried, she was so happy.

My sister is a senior in high school. She's not a dummy. She's a very smart person. She's also very caring about people. She just didn't see why I was getting the birthmark taken off. "It doesn't bother you, does it?" She doesn't have something like that. All your life and finally getting the opportunity to be able to end the problem. Just like somebody who's blind may have a cornea transplant and be able to see now. So somebody with a bad heart they've had all their life now may be able to live a normal life. People don't realize what it's like to have that hope. My sister has very big upper teeth. She does. They protrude. She won't get braces. She's afraid she'll look funnier with the braces. But when she smiles, she smiles with her lip down over her teeth. "Now you know how I feel," I tell her.

I'll tell you a story of a man who lives in Media. He is in his sixties. He has a birthmark on his face. It's a lot darker than mine. He's been using Lydia O'Leary cosmetics. It's a line of cosmetics for birthmarks, burns, bad scars, mostly for the face. It's a cover-up. He ran out of the cosmetic. He would not get on the trolley because he couldn't cover up the birthmark. He was that self-conscious of it. He walked from Media to Center City, Philadelphia, about fifteen miles, to Gimbels to buy what he needed. He wouldn't get on public transportation. He saw more people on the street, but it was a quick thing. He could walk right by them.

I wore a cosmetic for two years. I don't like it. When a girl wears it, she wears a base with some rouge over it and it covers it. It just looks like she's wearing facial makeup. Whereas, when I was wearing it, I was self-conscious that people would make fun of me because I was wearing makeup. I don't need it. I don't have the time for it. I don't really want it. I got it easy compared to others. Somebody that's blind. They do for themselves, but they don't do everything for themselves. I drive Carolyn to work every morning at 7:00. There's a girl that stands on the corner. She can't see when she can cross—it's a flashing yellow light. The cars don't slow down, so who's going to stop? So I roll down my window and I wait. When there's no cars, I say, "Go ahead, hon, it's clear."

Where I got it easy, I got full use of all my senses. I got my hands and my feet. I can walk and talk. I can hear and see. Where they can't. *This* is minor.

Ken's message. It's nice now that people are getting the handicap stickers, parking spaces. People park there anyway. They don't care. They get out of the car and fake a limp. Lay off. Let people have their three spots out of the 900 in the parking lot. Let them have it. The buses now have special ramps; the stores must have restrooms the handicapped can use. I think it's great. Anybody that's handicapped would rather do for themselves than let somebody help them, but there's a lot of things they can't do. And help that they need is not always there.

Be a little more caring. *Hear that, everybody!* [shouts into the tape recorder]. It's true. If people were a little more caring—not necessarily about a handicapped person—but everybody, we wouldn't have the problems we have.

MILDRED
(A Cosmetic Representative)

Mildred has a port-wine birthmark covering the right side of her face. She and her daughter Lydia were fixing breakfast during the interview. Her daughter said she never knows who she will find in the kitchen. People visit and call from all over the United States asking for help with cosmetic problems. Mildred is a promoter of Covermark, a product that covers blemishes. She speaks to nurses, doctors, vocational schools, and is interviewed for newspapers and magazines. She demonstrates the use of Covermark.

I feel Covermark is a gift of God. I don't think of it as just a commercial product. It is a means to an end—just like a wheelchair is a means to an end. Without the wheelchair, you couldn't move; without the Covermark, you could not meld into the group. Psychologically, if you are handicapped and have to wear a special boot to make you walk straight, or use a cane or a crutch, it helps you along life's way. I think of a corrective makeup in the same sense. We are basically interested in the psychology of acceptance. Regardless of what the problem is, you have to accept these means to an end. Before you can accept these helps, you first have to accept yourself.

[Mildred answers a phone call. The daughter goes on talking.]

I resent your being here today. I am feeling very hostile. I don't think of my mother as handicapped. I see people who are beautiful, intelligent, and to me they're more handicapped mentally and spiritually than anybody who has a physical handicap. I'm not feeling hostile directly at *you*. I'm feeling hostile because I do resent people staring at my mother. Because she doesn't have a handicap, really.

She has such a good-hearted personality. I think people take advantage of my mom because of her birthmark. She's a very kind, loving person. I guess she has a lot of empathy for mankind. Growing up, she had a hard time. When she was a little kid, kids made fun of her. She has a lot of empathy which I don't have because I didn't have to deal with it. She'll help people without money just to make them feel good about themselves. I resent that. She's given a lot away. She's given of herself. She says she's gotten back, not materially, but in self-satisfaction. She has people coming in since I was a kid—like *this* [indicating my presence at the table]. I would get up and strangers would be there. I just resent it. That's my mom's personality. It's her life and she does what she wants.

She's made her life around her so-called handicap. My name is Lydia. I'm named after Lydia O'Leary, the creator of Covermark. She's my godmother. I've sort of been dragged into it.

I'm always more embarrassed if I go out in public with my mother and she doesn't have her makeup on than *she* ever was. Because I get hostile. She never feels that. People look at her or they look *away*. They don't want to hurt her feelings. Little kids look at her because little kids are innocent.

[Mildred returns after talking on the phone to a man from New Jersey who needs advice because he has developed red blotches on his neck from overexposure to the sun. She resumes talking.]

There is such a need for people to realize that we are all made up of pigment, hair follicles, and capillaries. What I have on my face is an overgrowth of capillaries that lay all the way through layers of skin. Maybe it's from bad genes [laughs]. They don't know the actual cause why one child should be born with a birthmark and one should not. We humans think we know it all and we know so little. It's an unfortunate thing that happened when I was conceived. Maybe God intended it to help others who acquire blemishes.

I'm not a counselor and I'm not paid to counsel, but naturally over the years, I have studied some psychology and I do understand human nature. I guess there's no one better, because it's very easy for people to communicate with me. I have as much need for correction and coverage as they do.

A man came to me with a small birthmark. He's a sensitive

spirit. If it wasn't the birthmark, it would be maybe the shape of his ears, the shape of his nose. He's fighting battles within himself. He is not aware that he's fighting battles and blames it on the outside reactions of people. *Until I give off vibes of strength and acceptance of self, I can't expect others to carry me.*

You look at someone like me and you say, "How did you feel when you were a little girl?" or "How did you feel when you were in high school?" or "How did you feel when you went to a party?" and I can tell you that there is a tempering of the sword through the entire life. The way I felt when I was a child, the way I felt when I was in grammar school, the way I felt in high school, when I had an inferiority complex, is not how I feel now. It is so much different than when I started to work. I was married when I was 25 to a man who knew me before I ever used Covermark. I'm still married. It isn't fair and right for people to read this and say, "That Mildred Kraft had a terrible complex and she's a noble soul. She was able to go beyond herself and do this work even with this sense of complex."

There are people like me who want to overcompensate. It's almost a part of their human nature. God plans in his own way. He gives you something to compensate.

I have found that 90 percent of handicapped people are the strongest, least handicapped people in this world because they *do* accept themselves. They are the giants of the world. If you want to compare a pea to an elephant, it's like saying this handicap—or visible difference—is like *nothing*. But the person with the greatest handicap could be the greatest spirit. The person with the very minor insignificant temporary acne problem could be so troubled with himself, that that could be the biggest handicap. Now that person could magnify that to a point where he honestly believes that if he has a pimple on the end of the nose, everyone is so concerned with him that all they see is the pimple on the end of the nose. Most people are not that interested in their fellowman. They're just looking at the person as a *whole*.

The person with the problem has got to understand that they have to, in their own way, build their protective shell. They build it by compensating—by being extra kind, extra good, extra pleasant, and they'll find that whatever they do comes back to themselves.

Her husband, Carl, walks in.

I think the reason I have so much love for Carl is because of his spirit. He doesn't see the birthmark—he sees beyond the birthmark. He doesn't try to analyze.

She brings out her photo book of before-and-after pictures of people who use Covermark.

Now here's Katherine. She's out in Michigan. Now she's an example. She had such a deep inferiority complex. When she got her first jar of Covermark, she would have her jar at her night table. She would wake up at night and make sure that jar of Covermark was still there. That's how Covermark very often allows people to accept themselves.

There are very few people who feel like I do. That's why I keep saying to God, "God, is this maybe my peace of mind?" He knew I couldn't work without that peace of mind. Maybe he *made* me like this to bring Covermark to people for comfort. This is what I like to think.

REBECCA (A Schoolgirl)

Rebecca has a birthmark with complications of the lower lip. I asked her how a fifteen-year-old young woman deals with adolescence while coping with a birthmark on the lower half of her face and swollen lower lip.

I cover my birthmark with Covermark makeup. My birthmark extends from under my nose to around my chin. My lip is part of the complication. That's why it's big, but I'm getting an operation done on it. I've had two operations, and I'll be getting another one this summer. It's not a series of operations. It's like they do it and they hope it works. The first one worked—it pulled it up. The second one didn't work at all. We are hoping that the third one works.

I was born that way. It was big when I was born. It got bigger as I got older. I guess I always hated it. As I got older, I just learned to cope with it.

When I was younger, kids used to tease me. Up to the fifth grade they teased me. Even now I meet an occasional person at school who is a pain and teases me. But it doesn't bother me. It's not like everyone does it, just one or two. Fifth grade was my hardest grade. The kids got on my case. I hated going to school. They would tease me about my lip. That was before my first operation, and it was bigger and they teased me a lot. They called me "Big Lip." I only had one friend, but they teased her, too, because she was fat. We would stay together. I would be late getting home from school because kids wouldn't let me in my locker, and I would just cry. I usually didn't tell my parents. I was embarrassed. *I kinda kept it in myself and buried it.* Me and my friend just kinda took it, but we hated it. When I told my mom that I hated it, she switched me over to Catholic school where I had a lot of friends. It was smaller and I liked it better. Then I went to O'Hara High School where I am now and I have a lot of friends.

I always wear my makeup to school. I don't think I would go

without it because I would feel weird. I wear makeup all the time, wherever I go. People wouldn't know I had a birthmark. They could see the lip, of course, but they probably would think it was from the braces.

As I was getting older, I started getting more self-conscious about it. I wear the makeup all the time now, but when I was younger I never wore it. There are two other kids my age in the neighborhood. We would just play together. I wouldn't bother about makeup and they wouldn't care. I would go over to their houses and they'd come here. As I got older, I wore it more and more. The last time I went without it was maybe in the fourth grade.

It's not hard to put on. I just hate getting up ten minutes earlier than everyone else. It's just a pain. It doesn't come off in my sports, even in swimming. But if I rub my hand across my nose while swimming, it does come off a little. If it comes off, I fix it. I carry little packets of makeup and I fix it.

I go out a lot

My lip is the biggest problem. The birthmark doesn't bother me near as much as my lip. I feel I always have to try a bit harder to find a boyfriend or a little bit harder to get a good friend. But I go out a lot. I'm choosy like every other girl would be. Before I went to high school, I always thought that I would never get a date. But it turns out that I was wrong. I do get dates. I even turn down a lot.

I hate it! But I have to live with it

A majority of people will ask me about my lip. I work in a hospital as a candy striper and a lot of people there ask. If I'm in a bad mood and I don't want to answer them, I will say, "I just got my braces on," or I'll say, "I was born like that." A lot of times, if I'm in a really bad mood, I'll just say *anything* to make them stop talking to me. Other times, if I'm in a happy mood and talkative, I will just babble on. I'll say, "I had a birthmark here. I was born with it and I've had two operations and I'm hoping to get a third this summer."

It bothers me to have people ask me. It makes me *more* self-conscious of it. It's hard to forget it is there and once I forget it, someone says, "Oh, what happened?" Then I'll remember it. I don't like it at all. *I hate it!*

I like people best when they just don't care about it—people who don't even notice it. They just start talking to me and they don't look at it or ask about it and they don't care. I sort of *expect* people to ask or look at it, but I *hope* to avoid the subject. People do try not to look at the lip. They'll look me in the eye or over to one side.

I *always* see it when I look in the mirror. I get angry at it, too. I always say, "Why am *I* different? Why *me*?" I think that a lot. I only wish it would just go away. People without a birthmark are lucky. They're very lucky. They don't have to get up every morning and put makeup on. They don't have to worry about fixing their hair up special every day so people will notice your hair, not your mouth or your birthmark. They're just really lucky.

Rebecca's message to those who are visibly different. Give yourself a high, don't let yourself drop. If someone teases you, don't get depressed. If you get depressed and you let them know you're depressed, they'll just keep doing it. Act like you're really popular. If you act like you're popular, you will become popular. Don't act snobbish. Be nice to your friends. Don't let anyone tell you what to do just because you're different.

If you're worried about getting a boyfriend, don't get wrapped around their finger. Don't do everything they want. It just won't work. It's better that you tell them off before they take advantage of you because they have you wrapped around their finger.

REBECCA'S MOTHER

Being the mother of a child with a visible difference carries its own load. Rebecca's mother gave me this interview over the phone.

When she was born and they told me about it, I was in total shock. I was just numb. After about ten minutes you immediately put it aside. My husband was sort of prepared because I explained it to him before he saw her.

The first question I asked the pediatrician was, "What did I do wrong?" All doctors gave me the exact same answer, "Nobody knows." *I had a feeling of guilt.* You go over every inch of your pregnancy—lots and lots of times—for fifteen years. I thought maybe it was because I'm a very active person and maybe I shouldn't have been so active when I was pregnant.

We did not put makeup on her until she was seven months old. After that, we put makeup on every time we went out. If she didn't have it on, oh, my, how people would stare—especially older people. The most difficulty is with senior citizens. They don't have to say *anything.* You get to know every trick in the book. You can pretty well tell what they're thinking. Some people *enjoy* looking. I really had to reconcile myself to the fact that our senior citizens are not what they are cracked up to be.

Covermark makeup is the best thing we have today. There are a lot of things wrong with it. It is so hot to wear. The summer is dreadful. If we're at the shore, it's awful. The extreme heat is an awful problem. She's a gymnast and she sweats. It does not take kindly to sweating. We *never* considered her not wearing Covermark. I don't know if I would subject her body to that kind of abuse. People stare at something that is unusual—that is an oddity. The first thing they see is your face. I don't know if *I* could handle it.

She has other problems stemming from the birthmark. The birthmark is on the lower half of the face and her lower lip continues to swell. She has had two surgeries on her lower lip. That is her problem. I know nobody at high school knows about her birthmark, but her lower lip continues to swell. She may have to have more surgery this summer.

You get no vacation from it

It is not a *minor* problem. It is a constant problem. I can just run out of the house without makeup any time I feel like it. She can't. Every day she must put on her makeup. There is not such a thing as rest. You have to make sure your face is perfectly clean every single night. You have to clean your skin perfectly. You get no vacation from it, ever.

There is no question of her going without her makeup. I think she has a lot of dignity. Why should she subject herself to having all her peers stare at her? Oh, no. I would never tell her to give up her makeup. If you yourself have never been with someone who has been stared at constantly, then you don't know.

She would have to be superhuman not to feel angry. "Why can't I be like everybody else?" These are natural reactions of frustration.

I don't know what she would be like if she didn't have the birthmark. I admire her. I don't know if I could be as outgoing and friendly as she is. She goes right ahead and does what she wants. She has a lot of "moxy." It takes a lot of courage. In war, men need courage once. But hers is every day. She has a lot more guts than anybody I know. When she plays field hockey, she knows some of that makeup will come off. She is distracted from what she is doing all the time. She is aware of the fact that when it comes off, people will look at her. You would be shocked if you saw it. If you had no warning, your face would register everything you're thinking. The one thing in life you want most is to look like everybody else. I can't expect people to accept me unless I look like everybody else.

I would take on the devil himself

I constantly shield her. Whenever we go to the shore, I constantly wonder if she will be put in a bad position for herself. Will there be a place she can repair her makeup? I still do this. I still walk in front of her. I cannot stop myself from walking in front of her first. Before people can stare at her, they have to look at me. I would make people stare around me. I would ask people if they have some question or ask what they are staring at. When I see someone looking at her and I see their line of vision, I pop my head in front of hers. People see my eyes asking them, "What are you doing?" Some people will actually change their position to see her. Even with the swollen lip, she is pretty. She has beautiful eyes. She has a beautiful figure.

Her message. I never find fault with people who try to accept. If you used makeup on your face to make yourself a little bit ugly, you would find a whole new world. You would find out things you never dreamed. You take on Rebecca's burden for one day. You go into the mall. You will have a sequel to your book.

KELOIDS

PAT (Housewife)

Pat explains that keloids is really an overgrowth of scar tissue. It is a condition that's peculiar to black people and some Caucasians of Mediterranean origin, Jewish people, and various other people with darker skins. It's something that recurs. A technique has not been perfected for removing keloids surgically without recurrence. Pat is a black woman who has had keloids on her arm and neck since age six.

As far as I can remember it stemmed from a childhood injury. I must have been about six. I was in the country in Maryland at my grandmother's for the summer. We saw the mailman and my cousin and I proceeded to race to get the mail first out of the box. She ran up to get the mail and I was threatening to pull her down. She kicked out at me and she didn't realize that I was quite that close. She had a loose plate on her shoe that cut me. That's originally how it happened. A growth occurred because of this injury. A doctor convinced my grandmother that this was some sort of growth that could be lanced. I remember them trying to remove it, but I don't remember them giving me anything to deaden the pain. They kept squirting something very cold on it and it was supposed to kill the pain. I can remember screaming and being held down on the table.

Pat learned about her condition by eavesdropping

I learned about keloids because I heard somebody say something about it. Evidently somebody had asked my mother and she was saying something about keloids and her father having had them. I used to listen. I was a quiet kid. I got to hear a lot of things because they didn't know I was around. That's basically how I knew what it was when I was a child. My mother never said anything about it.

I always knew it was there, but it didn't make me feel really different during elementary school. It was just a small place, just on my neck. I can't remember any of the children really talking about it or setting me aside as different or taunting me about it. I probably first became aware of it when I was well into my teens. I was raised in North Philadelphia. People were very close there and there were neighborhood schools. When you went to school, you basically knew everybody anyhow. It was very rare that a stranger came in. Therefore, I was just one of the gang around there and it didn't bother me.

Of course, as I got older I was interested in having it removed. My mother and father, through another person in the family, had learned of a surgeon at Temple [University] Hospital who claimed to be able to remove it. It was a new technique. I had to have Xray after Xray. It was okay for a while and then it recurred. Once they do it, it's just like a normal incision and then over a period of time it begins to puff up again. That didn't work.

After I was married, this same aunt told me about a friend of hers who also had a keloid on her throat and she had gone to Graduate Hospital and an Indian doctor there had removed it. He had not sutured it and this thing had never recurred. I went down to Graduate Hospital and I talked to them about it. He performed the same technique on me and cautioned me about not stretching my neck. For the longest time I walked around just staring straight ahead or turning my whole body. Originally it had been just a little spot. But something caused him to spread out the incision and therefore when it did finally recur, after maybe two and a half years, it was that much larger and it spread.

My daughter was severely burned in a fire and she had

massive scarring. Evidently keloids are passed down in families. She was at Shriners' Hospital for Children and they excised the scars surgically and gave her injections of steroids. After I saw how well it did, I began to get steroids. But she was younger and her scars were more pliable because they were new. But with me it was such an extremely painful thing. My face would puff up. After a while I noticed I'd become very depressed and I'd cry. Besides other things going on in my life, I had to go there every week and have five injections in my face! I just couldn't take any more of it so I stopped. But it did reduce it considerably and it was years before it began to grow again.

It never bothered my husband. Sometimes husbands and wives become angry at one another and say things to hurt. Well, that never came up. It didn't bother him evidently. I really became aware of it when I separated from my husband and I was by myself. I was just then really getting out into the social swim. Basically I had been in a tightly sheltered little world. When I was out there, there was the competition between women for the various men that were available. I really became aware of it then. And in having to go to work out of my own area, because I was strange to other people. I found also the scarring had become much more intensive than when I was younger. When it gets to be a larger thing, it's something really different and people tend to stare.

I've never really had to pursue men. It seemed as though they were always pursuing me and I've had more than my share interested in me. I have a keloid on my arm also from a vaccination. I never wear sleeveless clothes even though I've more or less gotten used to people seeing the one on my face. I just somehow have strong reservations about both of them showing at the same time. Now *that* bothered me when it came to a relationship with a new man because I said, "Well, he knows about this one, but how's he going to feel when he discovers that I have this on my arm?" I guess I was just lucky in finding intelligent men—well, they didn't have to be so intelligent, but anyway, they never said anything about it.

The person that I was most involved with, the one I really cared the most about, went out of his way at times to show me that it didn't matter to him. There were times when I would be very apprehensive about going into any crowd, like a party or something like that. *I just felt that every time I went into a new situation, that I'd have to make that adjustment until they got used to me.* Sometimes I'd want to stay home. He would always tell me that I would have to go and there was no reason for me to stay home, that I had to make myself go even when I didn't feel like it, and that I would enjoy myself once I got there.

I have found that sometimes women have been very catty about it, but that hasn't bothered me. One was a girl that I worked with and she was very interested in a fella that was there. She was sitting, talking to this fella, and I came into the room. He stopped talking to her and turned around and started holding a conversation with me. She yelled out very loudly, "Oooo." And she made a terrible face. She said, "Oh, that scar on Pat's face is so horrible. And you see the hair growing on it." I just looked at her and I said, "You know, it's a good thing that I'm not sensitive about it, because you have no tact. You're crude, you know, you're ignorant. You don't do things like that to people." But then I said, "I think I know where you're coming from, anyway. I'll leave you to your conversation."

I wonder if they'll hire me

I've been lucky getting jobs. I did go through skullduggery once to get a job in a hospital. It was just as a tray girl. I wore a scarf. I just wrapped the scarf around my neck and when I was interviewed I never took off the scarf or my coat. The dietician who hired me sort of started the first time she saw me without the scarf but didn't say anything to me. I had to take the trays into the rooms and put them down at the bedside. I worked for a month and then one day she met me in the hall. She said, "Would you mind wearing a mask, a surgical mask, when you go into some of the patients' rooms?" Evidently someone had said something to her. I said, because I had four kids to take care of, "Well, it's the mask or the job." She gave me the mask and yet I don't know if she discussed it with someone else, or she decided that it was ridiculous or what, but they never made me wear it. I felt sort of hurt, crushed. I was sort of dejected about the whole thing, but then I remembered that I had really tricked them into giving me the job. I didn't stay there too long anyway, because I didn't like the attitude there. You were just treated as though you were on the plantation, if I might be frank.

There was a time when I went for an interview and I was really hurt. It hurt me for a long time, then the hurt went away and I got extremely angry. I used to sit around and plot about going around and doing things to them. I answered an ad in the paper for a drugstore. I walked in there. The druggist just looked at me and said, "You can't have the job." I said, "Why? You haven't even interviewed me." He said in this awful loud voice, "I can't hire you with a face like that." I left the store in tears.

Other than that, I don't think that it has affected my jobs. It didn't seem to be a problem. Co-workers? They didn't make any particular distinction. I think it was just a matter of looking at me once and seeing it, and then you're just somebody who works there.

I'd like to be a nurse. But then I wonder will they hire me, because some people are very funny. I would like most of all to be an obstetric nurse. But you know some women are very superstitious about marking babies and all that kind of stuff. If after talking to various administrators in the hospitals, if the reaction seems to be negative, then I'm not going to waste my time or the money trying to go to school.

I dread children

Children seem to pay more attention than anybody. I dread children. Not so much a child that I'd meet on familiar surroundings, but if I'm on a bus or in a department store, all of a sudden a kid yells out, as only they can, "Mommy, what's that thing on that lady's face?" and every head swivels around and looks at me. I've always been a shy person. I'm basically a loner, an introvert. I think it's my basic personality and I always hated to be stared at. I've had it happen to me several times and sometimes the mothers don't even say anything. Sometimes the mothers actually turn around and stare themselves. So what can you expect from a child when you see that? Consider the source.

Aside from children, adults don't usually bother me. Sometimes I might even get a little mean about it because I'm sort of impatient with nonsense. Today when I was on the el [elevated train], a woman kept looking at me, and she grabbed her throat and kept staring at me. She wasn't saying a word. When I got up—and she was sitting right next to the door—I just walked over to the door and I stared down at her and said, "Lady, why are you holding your throat?" She was so embarrassed she never even answered and I just got off chuckling to myself. I said to myself, "Well, now she's embarrassed. Serves her right."

Sometimes I don't feel like being bothered with nonsense and I want them to know what it feels like to be inconsiderate of other people. I have seen things that were unusual on people. You try not to look at the floor and make a spectacle of not looking at them because that's just as obvious as staring at them. It's unfortunate, but they're human beings and they deserve to be treated just like anybody else. But some people are just very inconsiderate. They don't know. Some of them are just ignorant.

Pat's Message. I have to do a lot of explaining and I'm sick of explaining the whole thing. I don't mind if you approach me in an intelligent manner and quietly. But sometimes I feel if somebody asks me one more time, I'll just scream. I want to be treated just like everybody else is treated.

ALOPECIA
(HAIRLESSNESS)

MIKE (A Service Representative)

I was in the car when I saw Mike jogging down the street. With his red warm-up suit and totally bald head, it was easy to keep track of him for the six blocks it took to chase him down. On finally flagging him and explaining my book about people with visible differences, he laughed and said, "So, what's so different about me!"

The technical term for it is alopecia. I lost my hair when I was twelve. I had a bald spot on the back of my head. It was called *alopecia ariata*, and I had that for a few years. Then all of a sudden, one day, I began losing more of my hair, and about a week to ten days later it was *all* gone. I was scared. I do remember that. I was very scared. I come from a good family and my family knew how to handle it. They were constantly pushing me out. It wasn't my personality to stay at home, but I was scared at first—but I was pushed out the door—which was good.

Other kids made fun of me—twelve year olds! [laughs] Kids are cruel—you know that. I'm sure I was just as cruel as a kid, too. No sympathy asked for, none needed. They made fun of me—still do—but now I enjoy it. Now I listen for the good ones.

There was a point in high school where I had to stand up and prove myself, kind of draw the line. I got involved in a lot of fights. "I'm not going to take any more." That's where I made my decision. I decided I'm a regular ole guy and I'm not gonna be the one laughed at sitting in the corner. It didn't make any difference to my true friends. I had as many friends as anyone else did. I can't even remember feeling, except maybe initially, that I was "different." I *knew* I was different, but I didn't *feel* different. I was just a guy without hair.

I even say to this day, I love the jokin' and messin' around. There's always good jokes about it. And I think that's part of it. I never get tired of it. That's great. That fits my personality. But what I *don't* like is when people try to *humiliate* me because of it. That's what I don't tolerate. I learned in my high school days the difference between joking—having a good time—and making a fool out of me, which to this day I don't stand for.

I didn't have a particularly difficult time. I come from a large family—seven kids. My mother was the boss. You couldn't go around feeling sorry for yourself. We weren't allowed to sit around feeling sorry for ourselves. You have to understand, I don't *feel* any different, especially now. I'll walk anywhere and hold my head high. I don't feel inflicted or anything. It's a good feeling I have toward it. If I had hair I think I'd cut it off right now. Or if it was glued back, I'd cut it off. It wouldn't be me. Even when I was a kid, my parents asked if I wanted wigs. I wouldn't be myself—that was always my standard answer.

This is me

Anywhere I go in the neighborhood, I'm noticed. Anywhere in Upper Darby I go, I'm noticed. Anywhere in Delaware County. We go anywhere and people say to me, "Weren't you in my house to fix my refrigerator?" or "I remember you from high school." Whereas, I don't remember the person that's sayin' it. 'Cause they've changed. And I haven't.

I love my work. I've been doing it for eleven years. I'm in business where I go into people's homes. I do service work. It got to a point a few years back where I was spending more time explaining to people why I was bald and why I didn't have any hair than I was explaining to them why their refrigerator didn't work. To a point where it was taking away from my job. They'd ask me all kinds of crazy questions. People are very blunt. "Where's your hair?" So what I do now, I wear a hat. The reason I wear a hat ... there's a couple of reasons. I work in tight spots and I get up and I cut my head or I bang my head. I'd get tired of walking around with scabs on my head so I wear a hat in the homes. Now that fulfills two purposes: I don't get scabs on my head anymore and people don't know that I'm bald. So they don't ask me. Or you catch them peeking under my hat [laughs]. Now I say I can't work without my hat. In fact, that's how I'm described at work. People will call up the office and they'll say, "It was the guy with the hat," or "The blond-headed guy with the hat," or "The guy with the light hair" [laughs].

It's the initial getting used to. When people get to know me, they say, "Hey, he's a regular guy, he just doesn't have to go to the barber." That's all. That's the only difference. I walk in the neighborhood where I grew up and people don't look at me twice. I couldn't care less if people look at me. That doesn't bother me. The only thing that bothers me is if I'm with my family and people make loud comments. I've been with the kids a couple times when they were younger. They'd say, "Daddy, why do they say that to you for?" Now they're older and they understand. It doesn't bother them. My kids used to pat me on my head.

[Wife interjects]: They wanted to comb his hair. When they were little, they would get a comb and comb it like they didn't know.

They just let it roll off. I don't think it bothers them. They haven't mentioned to me that it bothers them.

I don't hear comments anymore. I think the age factor has something to do with it. We're not teenagers anymore. I referee basketball here in Upper Darby. I referee ages between twelve and twenty. I hear the comments constantly—but they're kids. They're with their own crowd.

They have to have something to talk about so they wait for opportunities like this. But they're not directed at *me*—they're just directed by someone trying to get a conversation going for themselves.

Co-workers...

I'm the biggest joke of the office meetings. Sure. That's part of the game. That's quite understandable. I know the guys at work can't wait to have meetings so they can joke on me. That's fine. Because I've got the personality for that, too. I can get my licks in [laughs].

Is there any place it's difficult for you to go?

The barbershop [big laugh all around].

The army was a rough experience. I was scared to death—but not about my hair. That was actually secondary. But there again that's the situation in the army where you're *living* with people and once you've got a day of living with a person, they don't look at you anymore. I was worried about getting *shot*—I wasn't worried about my hair.

Is it inherited?

No. There's not a bald-headed person in the family. My father is 55 years old and still has all his hair. Personally, I feel my mother made the discovery after all the doctors failed, and I kind of agree with her. I had an aunt who died, followed closely by my grandfather. I was very close to him. We kind of have a feeling it was a shock to the system more than anything. I believe that theory more than the specialist who charges $35, $50 every ten minutes to tell you how you were nervous. If your nerves weren't bad when you started with them, they're sure you're gonna have bad nerves when you're through with them.

I've been through experiences with doctors. I was at a dermatologist convention. I don't know if you have any idea what they're like. It was like a freak show. They'd just get everybody in different cubicles and doctors would come in and stare. That was one of the most humiliating things I've ever been to. The dermatologist I was going to. . . . I'll never forget [him]. He used to come in and stare at my head and go, "Hmmm, hmmm." One time, this is what finally ended it, they stuck needles in the side of my head and it looked like somebody stuck an orange or a very big ball between my skin. I walked around with a lump. It hurt. It hurt bad. That's when I finally said to my parents, "I'm not going back." They didn't tell me why they did this needle bit or anything. They were getting my father's money.

I have to say that I've said, "Why me?" but isn't that a normal reaction? I went to Catholic school, and my parents— especially my mother—she's super religious to this day. I was involved a lot in praying and stuff like that. I can remember making deals in my head. "If you give me hair, I'll do this. . . ." You know what I mean.

But I never blamed anyone. We weren't allowed. You have to understand that. My mother is a pretty tough person and we weren't allowed to do that. I guess she had a lot to do with my attitude now.

I think it bothered my father more than it did her. He'd probably tell you, no. He'd never give me a straight answer. There's nothing to talk about now. That's what you have to understand—there's nothing to discuss. I come from a very large family and there's more important things to discuss. There's no problem.

AL* (Unemployed)

The front of Al's shirt reads, "God made only a few perfect heads. On the rest he put hair." Although Al is in his early thirties, he is completely bald. He started losing his hair and decided it would look better if he shaved it all off.

After I was married, we came back from Indiana to start a business here in Upper Darby. It was just about the time that hair was starting to get long. I noticed that the hair was coming out along the bottom of the hairline—across the back, over the ears where the sideburns are. As it got worse, I just let my hair grow. I let it grow down to cover it over. I went to a dermatologist and he said it was alopecia, which is attributed to nerves as far as they can tell. He gave me some medication which was brown and ugly and smelled. It was a petroleum based product that I rubbed in. Eventually some of my hair came back.

So I just shaved it all off

It started coming out after I had been diagnosed as having sarcoidosis.** I was taking strong doses of different types of medication: Pregnazone, Librium, and a number of other various and assorted things. It got to the point where I looked like I'd been in a fight. Like somebody had just grabbed handfuls of it. The thought of looking half and half really bothered me and I figured it was easier to take care of it and it would look better if I just took it off. So I shaved it off. I went down to my barber and we just spent an hour in the chair. We just shaved all kinds of designs into whatever was left. We had a grand time with it and he never charged me for doing it when the thing was over. Now I shave maybe once a week.

*After asking Al for an interview, I discovered he also has multiple sclerosis. (See pages 72-78.)

* *later diagnosed as multiple sclerosis

I guess I was into my thirties by then. I had been working for a while. It didn't affect my work. Obviously there was shock in the beginning because I did have a very good head of hair. I asked my boss before I shaved it off. Obviously I asked my wife before I did it. She told me the only way she would ever divorce me is if I went bald. Just teasing. People say, "Why didn't you get a rug?" And I just couldn't see any sense to it. That's the way I was. I'm obviously not an introvert so I figured I'd be able to handle it. I tend to wear hats in the winter when I never did before because it does get a little cold without the hair on top of it. Other than that, there's no problem.

Reactions are strange. I tend to ignore people's reactions. Normally I don't let it bother me. I tease the kids. I see little kids in the supermarket. They look at me. A little boy said to his mother one day, "He doesn't have any hair." I rubbed the top of my head and said, "No. I guess I don't. I thought I had it when I left the house this morning." It's funny to them. Most people don't even care. Yul Brynner's been around for a while and Telly Savalas was around for a while. There was a period of time where people were shaving themselves bald for fashion. I guess most people don't care. My friends were a little surprised in the beginning, but it's still me. Once you get past that part of it, the me is still there.

I look like Daddy Warbucks

I look like Daddy Warbucks in a tuxedo. My daughter bought a shirt for me that I really like, "God could only make a few perfect heads so he put hair on the rest of them." It's cute. It's there. There's no way to hide it. I'm outgoing. It's a sign of expression. As far as I can, I try to make it easier on the kids 'cause it sometimes tends to scare them. I'll make jokes about it. It's just something that happened and you can decide that you want to put up with it, or you don't want to put up with it. If you don't, that's too bad 'cause there's nothing you can do about it anyway. Just let it go as it is. It's the same attitude I have toward the MS. People like my family, friends, just can't believe I've got the attitude that I have. I just have to live with it. In fact, it's easier to get dressed in the morning the way it is.

Al's message. I was brought up a lot differently than other people. I'm not prejudiced. I don't have hates. I don't have dislikes. I look at people for what they're worth. There's good and bad in all kinds. It doesn't matter. My judge of a person is the way they interact with me. I think I've been uncomfortable sometimes with people because they're different, but that's a normal reaction. I've never let it stand in the way of making decisions or interacting with people. I just wish that other people were like that.

ALBINO (PARTIALLY SIGHTED)

JAN* (Institutional Administrator)

Jan has strikingly light hair and a white complexion. In her forties now, she tells some of the difficulties she had in childhood due to her lack of knowledge about albinism.

Albinism is inherited. It's like anything else that's inherited. You can look in your family and you can trace it back. After you trace it back for a couple generations, it just disappears. That's what happened in our family. We don't know of anybody on my father's side of the family [with albinism] at all. My mother was one of five girls. There were three of them who were partial albinos and two who were not. Their vision is a bit better than mine and their hair has much more color than mine. Their hair is sort of yellow, not a bright yellow, but a nice soft yellow. Their skin has a little bit more color.

I have a sister who is albino just like I am. Many people thought we were twins. She is two years older than I, so she was always a bit bigger than I during childhood, but we looked so much alike. Sometimes our mother dressed us alike. When we grew up and walked down the street, people often asked if my sister, my mother, and I were triplets.

Becoming aware of my albinism was a whole process. It didn't just happen. My mother took us to the Indiana University Medical Center. We were hospitalized in the Children's Hospital. I don't know whether they didn't know

———
*Jan is also interviewed in chapter 5.

about albinism or just what, but they kept us there for three days of tests to try to determine what was wrong. A couple of years later we were in there for another couple of days of tests. My mother said that nobody ever told her that the problem was albinism and what that meant. They just said we didn't see well. Back in those days doctors didn't really explain much to parents. *And parents didn't feel they had the right to really insist on knowing either.*

The first time I heard about the albinism was when I was in the sixth grade. My mother didn't know anything about it [albinism] until I came home and told her this story: We had gotten two white mice for a nutrition experiment in our class. We were all oohing and ahing. How cute—but they're still mice [laughs]. At recess, one of my best friends came and said, "Janice, there's something about you like those white mice." It really hurt my feelings. I didn't understand it. I went to the teacher and said, "Why is everybody saying I look like the white mice?" He said, "Because of your white hair and your red eyes." I didn't know my eyes were red, or pink, ever before. That was an additional hurt.

I don't see eye color—not mine or anybody else's. Most people tell me they don't look pink or red, but when I was a kid, people often told me. Maybe they looked more pink when I was a child. I think that my glasses were almost always pink. Maybe that exaggerated the color of my eyes. When I look in the mirror, it looks to me like my eyes are sort of pale blue. People tell me now that they sort of change from being pink to grayish blue. I think it depends on the color tint in the glasses and the way the light is shining on my eyes.

It was the first time I heard the word albinism, and, of course, I had it all mixed up with mice. White rabbits and white mice, they're both furry and nice, but they're still rabbits and mice. The word "albinism" has some real negative connotations to it. All I needed was for somebody to come along and say, "You're like a mouse," to really top off my great inferiority complex. I talk to parents of albinos now. I tell them that from the time the child can first understand it, use the word "albino" and make it something positive. Don't use it just in connection with mice and rabbits. *I think it's this old thing that Americans have about differences.* Any difference is a bad difference.

Do you see in the dark?

One of the strange ideas is, if you're albino you can see in the dark almost like a cat. I've had some total strangers coming up and asking me things in very unkind ways. One time I was in a Horn and Hardart's, and the cashier said, "Do you see in the dark?" She said it so abruptly and crudely. I said, "No, do you?" When I was in college, I was in the library looking in the card catalog. Somebody came up, tapped me on the shoulder, and said, "Turn around and look at me." I did it out of shock, and she turned around and walked away. Maybe she wanted to know if my eyes were pink or red. I was hurt, angry, and insulted. How dare a total stranger come up out of the clear blue sky, just order me around, and not give me an explanation!

I remember one guy who was going to kiss me good-night. Instead he said, "Why are your eyes pink?" That's pretty devastating! My albinism isn't a problem for my husband. He's a very intelligent person who's very well read. He knew what albinism is, so I didn't have to do a lot of explaining to him. I had to explain what the implications for me were.

I made up my mind when I was a teenager that I didn't want to have children. The reason was because I was working through this thing about albinism. It was hereditary and I felt that I didn't want to have any children who were albino—which says an awful lot about how I felt about my albinism at that time. Since then my brothers and sisters have all had children. Their children have had children and their cousins have had children and nobody has had the albinism. Of course, at that time I didn't have that assurance. Still, I believe I could be the one who would have an albino child. I also feel strongly that mothers ought to stay home and take care of their kids. I made up my mind when I was a teenager that I was going to be a career person.

At one point I blamed my parents because albinism is hereditary; it was their fault. But then I was smart enough to know that they didn't know anything about albinism. I've gone through times when I've blamed God, but I don't think I've been bothered by that very much.

I guess I turn it around the other way. I've gotten things in life through this albinism that I wouldn't have gotten. Going to college is one thing. My parents never could have afforded to send me to college. I don't think I'm smart enough that I could have walked off with all kinds of scholarships to get myself through. But because I had a visual problem, State Rehab sent me through college. *I've worked at turning the albinism into a positive thing in my life.* I learned that from the black movement. I always thought it was such an inferior thing. But I learned from the black people that you can take something that's been regarded by yourself and society as bad and turn around and say, "Yeah, there's nothing inherently wrong with this. It's wrong because we say it's wrong."

Jan's message. Don't make judgments about people because they're different. Don't get scared because of the difference.

Another message I would have to handicapped people and professionals is about acceptance. It is expected that we go through a process where we accept our handicap and then forever after we've accepted it. It doesn't work like that. I've had some experiences myself where I think that I've worked this thing through and all of a sudden something else comes up. I get angry all over again. That's pretty normal for anybody who has a handicap, or any kind of difference. You get it all worked out at one point in your life. Suddenly there's a new experience and it just pops up again for no reason at all. You must experience the anger and frustration all over again.

4. HEARING Everybody's Got Something

The feelings and attitudes of the public toward those who are different from the majority group is an area for investigation in and of itself. In this regard often it is beneficial to think of the hearing impaired as a minority group. They are subject to biases and prejudices because they are different from the usual, the typical, and the familiar.

> —Helmer R. Myklebust,
> The Psychology of Deafness

If you're introduced as hard of hearing, people sort of freeze. They look uncomfortable. They're scared. Scared to death of you—you can see it in their eyes. They're scared of communicating with you.
> —Betty

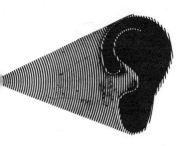

DEAF
AND
HARD OF HEARING

Technically, being deaf is not being able to hear sound until it is over 90 decibels (equivalent to a noisy factory or loud orchestral music). Practically, deafness means not being able to use a hearing aid for conversation or information without the assistance of lipreading or sign language. Deafness can be caused by heredity, birth trauma, sickness, accident, or aging. The vocal cords of a deaf person are not affected; therefore, the correct term is "deaf," not "deaf-mute." There are several methods of communication with the deaf. Fingerspelling uses the fingers to spell out the letters of each word. Oralism involves the use of speech and lipreading. Sign language uses hand and arm movements for words or phrases. Manual communication is a combination of fingerspelling and sign language.

Parents must choose a method of communication for their deaf child. The experiences of those interviewed may be of value in making a determination among the diverse methods.

Questions are answered relating to mainstreaming. Should children be placed in a "normal" learning atmosphere with special tutoring, or can they learn and adjust more efficiently in a residential or day school for the handicapped? The reader will find a surprising unanimity of opinion among those interviewed.

There is an unexpected acceptance of being deaf. "My deafness is a blessing. I don't have to hear that terrible music kids listen to now. I'm spared an awful lot of filthy language. I can do my work without being distracted" (Ginger). "I prefer to be deaf" (Marion).

Hard of hearing is a category between a mild hearing loss of 30 decibels (equivalent to a whisper) and a severe loss of 70 to 80 decibels (equivalent to a very loud radio). A hard of hearing person can communicate through speech with the use of a hearing aid. The hard of hearing must contend with the problems of misunderstanding, fear, anger, and impatience.

DEAF

GINGER
(An Administrative Assistant)

It was quiet in Ginger's house even though the TV was turned on. Her husband, who is also deaf, was watching it without sound as we talked. Ginger is the mother of three hearing children, an administrative assistant for supplies for a group of lawyers, and an active church woman in an Episcopalian church for the deaf. Ginger spoke and signed while I simultaneously repeated her message into the tape recorder.

I had spinal meningitis when I was five. It was during World War II when most of the penicillin was going to the armed forces. I was in a coma for a while. When I woke up, I didn't know I had been sick—just like a cold or something. When grandmother and my mother came into the room, they seemed to be talking, but I thought they were whispering. It got me furious. I thought they were playing a trick—all that whispering and I couldn't understand them. It was very frustrating. I had never heard the word "deaf" and I didn't know any deaf people. I didn't know what happened. It was a long time before I trusted my family after that.

I had a self-conscious feeling of being betrayed by them. I thought they were playing games on me. I found out in a month or so that it was *me* that was not hearing, not them that were not talking. Even after I found out I couldn't hear, I had a lingering feeling they weren't on my side.

I remember, a little later, I was taken to the doctor and my grandmother wrote things down that the doctor said. It was frightening because people were talking about me, deciding things about me. I felt mad about it. I felt I had a right to say something. I didn't have any say about myself.

It was still me

I had started school before I lost my hearing. I was still in the beginners class in a country schoolhouse when I became deaf. I had started school when I was four because my birthday is at the end of September. In November I got a sore throat. The doctor said my tonsils had to come out. After that I got pneumonia as a complication from the surgery. I got spinal meningitis three months after that. I didn't get much schooling that year.

When I was sick, the teacher came to my house and gave me lessons at home. My grandmother had been a teacher. She had taught me to read when I was three and I knew my numbers up to 100 and I could subtract and add. It was very lucky because if I had not been able to read when I lost my hearing, it would have been rough. I went back to the school for the last six weeks of the year and returned to first grade the next fall. It worked out pretty well. There were small classes. The teacher had four or five beginners, maybe a dozen or so in first grade, maybe ten or twelve in second grade. They put me in the front row. The teacher depended more on written tasks. We only had to get up and read when it was our turn in the book.

My mother took me to the Columbia Presbyterian Hospital in New York City. My grandfather was a doctor and he thought they should see me at a medical center because he thought maybe something could be done. I was in the children's ward. There was this nurse. I don't know what she thought she was doing. She would not write to me at all. She would just talk to me. If I didn't understand her, she slapped me. It was awful. There was a speech teacher there. She was nice. I thought we were playing games. She would write things down. She understood what she was trying to do.

When I was halfway through first grade my mother heard about Lexington School for the Deaf in New York. She took me down there after Christmas. She took me out again at the end of the year because the children were terribly ill-mannered. They were letting big kids take care of the little kids. I guess they were shorthanded. My mother said I was picking up all kinds of rudeness. She wouldn't have it. She put me back in the country school.

I hated the Lexington School for the Deaf. The kids were hard of hearing and I'm deaf. When I couldn't lip-read, the teacher would say I wasn't paying attention. If you didn't lip-read, then you were automatically naughty. The kids who were really deaf couldn't hear anything from the earphones. When the deaf couldn't hear, the teacher said they weren't paying attention. They weren't trying. I hated it so bad.

I had many friends in our small town. I walked home almost every day with a little girl who lived across the street from us. We had a lot of fun. There was another girl whose mother let us put a blanket over a line and make a tent. We played in that all the time. Another girl up the road had a playhouse. Her mother would let us have some soda in the little teapot and have a tea party. Another girl's mother had a shop in the back room and would let us play permanents and we would sit under the dryers. We had a lot of fun.

My whole family learned to fingerspell

The middle of third grade, after Christmas, my mother took me to the Rochester School for the Deaf. I stayed there until I finished high school. I didn't like it much. I'm a farm girl. I don't like cities. I didn't like being away from my family. It was 250 miles away and there were no thruways or turnpikes. It took about seven or eight hours to make the trip. I went to school after Christmas and I didn't go home until Easter. I went back [to school] after Easter and didn't go back [home] till summer. It's wrong for little kids.

They use fingerspelling at the Rochester School. They push

language skills—written, spoken, or spelled. I liked my teachers. I liked the housemothers. But I didn't like the other kids so much. I'm not very athletic. The kids were very athletic. If a ball comes at me, I don't catch it, I duck. I was very small for my age. I was a bright kid. At the Rochester School they put competitive groups in the same grade. I was with kids who were four or five years older than I was in class. I had learned to read at an early age and I was advanced in reading. I had good math skills. So I was in class with kids who were considerably older than I was. I liked to sit in a quiet corner and read while others went to the gym every chance they got. I got good marks and that didn't help my popularity any. It was embarrassing. Kids can be so mean. They don't mean anything by it, but they are.

My whole family learned to fingerspell. My mother, my grandmother, both my aunts, my sister, some of my cousins, one of my uncles. One of my uncles had arthritis and couldn't move his hand that good. But everybody in my family fingerspells. They learned for me. When I first lost my hearing, my mother went to a priest. He was a very wise man. Father Diamond told my mother, "Look, Margie, your daughter is going to have to learn to live with hearing people, but the most important thing is never to let her feel she is left out of the family. If she feels part of the family, she'll be able to manage okay in life." So my mother figured the way to make me feel completely part of the family was for them to learn to fingerspell. This was a long time before parents of the deaf children started organizing. At that time, schools for the deaf taught parents *not* to fingerspell or sign to their children.

Definitely parents should learn fingerspelling. If you couldn't communicate with your child, where would you be? How would you discipline your child? How would you discuss ethical questions? *You* talk to your kids all the time—you read to them, you sing to them. Your children help themselves to candy in the store. You make them take it back. You couldn't do all that if you didn't communicate with your kids.

You'd be slapping them all the time and they wouldn't know why. That's criminal. If the child is really deaf, you are hitting the kid for reasons he doesn't understand. He'll just turn around and slap other people. That's why so many deaf people break away from their families. They don't know the families care that much about them because they don't know how to reach out and communicate.

Fingerspelling is easier to learn than sign language because you're only learning one thing—the alphabet. It's better for the language of the deaf child. When you sign, you don't sign the endings, the tense, the plurals. You don't sign prepositions, conjunctions. When you fingerspell, you fingerspell the whole sentence—the correct tenses, and all the rest. But it's hard on the eyes from a distance.

You can see I am definitely anti-oralism. I've got many scars from it—from the hospital and Lexington School. I think it's just plain mean to make a little kid live up to a standard of speech or lipreading. A kid isn't ready for that kind of thing. I am not against speech. I am not against lipreading. I am against pushing them to where it is more important than the child's well-being.

I felt good in college

I felt very good in college. It was the first time I could remember people were not judging me by the fact that I was deaf, but letting me be myself. Gallaudet* was wonderful that way. In residential schools for the deaf they try to push you into a mold. All the kids wear the same uniform, take a bath Tuesdays and Thursdays, brush their teeth at the same time. There isn't room to be an individual. If you're an individual, you usually get in trouble. At Gallaudet they didn't have that many rules. There were more rules then than there are now, but it wasn't as regulated. I didn't notice my deafness at all because everybody was deaf. They let me be myself. Gallaudet is really

---

*Gallaudet College for the Deaf in Washington, D.C.

great that way. They let you find out who you are. I had friends at Gallaudet, Bob [her husband] for one. Most of my friends now are people I met at or through Gallaudet.

Why is she telling me what to do?

Theoretically, I am an administrative assistant for supplies. Most of the people over me don't seem to bother much about my being deaf. If I don't understand something, they say, "Wait a minute," and write it down. Some of the people I have to boss started being kind of defensive about it. If this person is deaf why is she telling me what to do? But that doesn't seem to be a problem any more. Only an initial thing: after they see you know what you're doing, they generally don't carry that kind of chip on their shoulder.

The church is very important to me

Telling you about my church work will take a while. To begin with, I was brought up in the Episcopalian Church. It was very high church. The only difference between me and the Roman Catholic Church is I don't believe the pope is infallible [laughs]. I am a lay reader. That means I assist the priest. I can conduct services—not communion. I am on the Altar Guild, one of the cochairmen. I am teaching new Altar Guild members now. I am in the choir. I often sign* the solos because I am not afraid to do the solos. No one interprets them unless there are hearing people there. Most of the congregation is deaf unless we have visitors. I am clerk of the church. I am chairman of the Evangelism Committee. I have been elected to the diocesan convention for the last four years. I am the only one who's not afraid to get up and say what I think in front of hearing people. All the other deaf people don't like to attract attention. I tell them it's their fault if they don't like the decisions. I am lay associate to a community of monks, and I'm also very

---

*Uses sign language. Solos in a church for the deaf are signed in a flowing manner rather than sung.

active in the healing ministry. That's very important to me.

Bob and I are very quiet people. We are both awful bookworms. We are introverts. We prefer to stay home. We like to have people come to dinner or to go to homes. But we don't like big parties—never have. We go to a ball game once or twice a year. We prefer to have a barbecue on our own back porch, invite one or two people to dinner. That sort of thing. We don't like a lot of social stuff. Most of our affairs are with other church people—meetings and socials. We don't really go to that many other things. We went to the Deaf Club. We didn't like it. It was so jammed. We couldn't breathe in there.

When there are parties or receptions, we make a token appearance and then come home. We go to family weddings, but that's really no big problem because all of my family can fingerspell. But we're not so comfortable around Bob's family because they are anti-manual communication. They want us to lipread. They can't understand that when you have eight or ten people, the conversation bounces around and you don't know who's speaking. They don't understand that and it's boring and frustrating. They forget to include us in the conversation.

I can't remember when I needed help in public. I'll tell you something. When we moved here five years ago, I was the first one to find my way around center city. All my kids couldn't find their way through the train station—and my kids can hear. They keep asking people for directions and following them and getting more lost. And I read directions on signs and find my way. Simple.

If I have to give an order or something like that in a restaurant or store, I talk. But if I want to make sure that the information got through, I write it down. The thing that bugs me most about being with people in public is if I'm shopping and somebody asks me some question and I don't catch it, I say, "I am deaf," and ask them to repeat it. They say, "Excuse me," and walk away. They couldn't expect information from a deaf person. It's very demoralizing. They act as if when you're deaf, you can't be depended on to tell them anything. That bugs me. People are not really *mean*. Most people are not overtly cruel. They just walk off because they don't know how to react. They're embarrassed.

One of the things that I hate is when we are in a mixed party in a restaurant. The waiter or waitress always picks some hearing person and then asks them what we want. Maybe they just don't know how to talk to us. After all, we're grown up. We can ask for what we want.

We had a doctor who, because I was deaf, wouldn't tell me anything. When we had our first baby, he decided our baby would naturally be deaf since my husband and I are deaf. He told us to wait a minute and he went down in the cellar and pounded on his furnace pipes. *I* could hear that. Our baby jumped. When he came up, I asked, "What did you do that for? Why didn't you ask me? I could tell you he jumps when I turn on the vacuum." He didn't ask because I'm deaf. I couldn't know anything.

I don't really think I want people to be especially kind to me. I just want to be treated like everybody else. I don't want anyone to fuss over me. That makes me uncomfortable. What I hate, the kind of person who comes over, "Oh, you poor thing," and brings me what I want. I could walk over and get it for myself. I'm not crippled, not mentally incompetent. I am not unable to pick up a cup of tea for myself. I just want to be treated like a normal person. I don't want people to go out of their way to accommodate my deafness. I don't want it rammed down my throat and made an object of pity.

Would you like to be hearing?

Heavens, no. Who wants that grief? Hearing people have my sympathy. I don't want ulcers. My deafness is a blessing. I don't have to hear that terrible music that kids listen to now. I'm spared that. I'm spared an awful lot of filthy language. When I was hearing, only some men used that language. Now women are using it. I'm just as glad I can't hear. I can do my work without being distracted. I'm not a slave to the telephone. When I see my boss with three or four telephone calls in ten minutes, I'm just as glad I don't hear that.

I have a very contemplative turn of mind. I am lay associate of a religious order. For a long time when I was younger, I wanted to be a contemplative nun. They didn't take me because I was deaf. I still have a lot of feel for contemplative prayer. I don't get disturbing noise in the street. I don't think I have the mental stress that many hearing people do. I don't have to listen to all the noise hearing people do when I'm trying to concentrate.

I know God had a reason for my deafness. I don't know what the reason is—but it is not punishment. It was necessary for his plan for me. I'm still trying to find out what his plan is. I find out little by little. It's just one of the things he needs to make his plan work. It doesn't concern me what plan he has. I'm just trying to work along with him. You just have to cooperate with grace.

Ginger's message. Take people for what they are, not for what labels they have on them. Just because a person is deaf or blind or retarded, that doesn't mean he or she can't be treated with respect. Everybody has a handicap. Every single person has at least one handicap. Some are racist. Some of us can't accept new ideas. Some are proud. Some have high blood pressure. My handicap is no worse. I'm sure my handicap is not worse than somebody who goes around tearing down other persons' lives. Look at the other person for themselves—what he or she *can* do. Don't judge from your concept of what he *should* do. I've wanted to say that for a good long time.

MARION (Retired)

Marion is a woman in her sixties who has been deaf from infancy. In the deaf senior citizens' lounge of a rehabilitation center, we sat across the table from each other with an interpreter. Marion told her story in sign language.

I was born deaf. When I was growing up, I didn't realize it. I have two hearing brothers and two deaf sisters. My parents were hearing. I used to wonder why I'm deaf and my brothers are hearing. My father just said, "You were born different." And then I understood.

My mother was afraid of the deafness. My father could accept it and treated us all the same. Mother did not. When I grew up, I could talk to my parents and they could understand me. Before that, I couldn't really talk good. My two brothers could understand me because they learned a little bit of sign language, too.

I was always in trouble (laughs). I used to sit on the train tracks and not hear the train coming. I'd sit there and play. A man had to grab me and I hit him. He told me the train was going past and I ran home. My father said I was a lot of trouble when I was small because I couldn't hear anything (laughs).

Did you have any problems going to stores or restaurants?

No. I would write on paper or my mother would write me a note and give it to me and I'd give it to the man. He'd read it and give me what I needed.

Were you afraid to go out in public?

No. I was not afraid to go to the store. If I knew the subject, I could talk pretty well on it.

Was the Pennsylvania School for the Deaf an oral school?

Yes. We had to lipread. We had to talk. We weren't allowed to sign. I like that. I think speech and lipreading is wonderful. I was in the choir at the school's chapel.

Which method do you think is best—oralism or sign language?

A long time ago oral was all right, but now it's hard. It's better to have sign, because then you have more knowledge than lipreading. Lipreading you can only understand some. You can't distinguish a *t* from a *d*, nor a *p* from a *b*. It's too hard. It's better if you have sign. You can pick up more. You can get more of what's going on. I like reading lips, I like signing, both.

Was there any particular age when it was difficult for you because you are deaf?

No, because I was always deaf. I was used to it. I did not have a hard time. I married a hearing husband and I talked and talked and used lipreading with him. I taught my husband sign language. He became *very* experienced at it. Very skilled.

If you got married again, would you marry a hearing person?

No. Deaf (vehemently). Because I can sign and talk and understand and get along. Hearing people, they don't know what you're saying.

What is your occupation?

I was a sewing machine operator. I enjoyed it—37 years I worked there. Then I retired. All of the people understood the deaf people. We never had any problems. There were two other deaf people. I worked with the hearing people, but I ate my lunch with the deaf people.

If you hadn't been deaf, is there another occupation you would have chosen?

I'd like to be a secretary. I'd get to wear nice clothes. It's a nice job. I could sit and type. I'd like to do that.

Are most of your social occasions with the deaf or with hearing people?

Deaf. I go to the Deaf Club. I go with other deaf people and play cards.

Are there places that you don't like to go?

The theater. The show's for the hearing.

When people see you on the street and want to talk to you, do you talk to them, or do you tell them that you're deaf?

I tell them I'm deaf, and I say to them, "What do you want?" and see if I can understand them or give them directions or anything.

Do most people continue talking to you or do they walk away?

Most of them walk away. When I say to them, "I can't hear. I am deaf." Most of them walk away. Maybe they have something against deafness, I don't know. Maybe they're afraid of the deaf. I don't know.

How do you feel when they do that?

Lousy. It makes me feel lousy. Hearing and deaf are the same. Why aren't they treated the same. I just feel lousy.

Do you ever get angry that you are deaf?

No. No. Not at all. I'm used to being deaf. I grew up that way.

Would you wish to be hearing?

No. I don't care. I don't really care. I'm old now anyway. I prefer to be deaf.

ERIC (Unemployed)

Eric is a personable, outgoing young man who was born deaf. Although he is out of school, he continues to take speech therapy in an effort to be better assimilated in the hearing community.

When I was a little boy. I was very frustrated. I didn't understand why I was deaf. I was wild. I remember my mother had a hard time with me—probably because I'm deaf. I was born deaf. I'm the only deaf person in my family. It scared my mother. I was very angry that I was deaf and I blamed it on my mother. I thought maybe she took pills or moved around too much while I was still in the womb. I don't blame anyone now. Now I understand. I thought it was only me. But there are many deaf people. That made me feel better.

My mother and father were divorced when I was still young. I didn't understand why. I said, "Where's daddy?" I thought my father didn't want me because I was deaf. My mother said, "No, there are problems between your father and me." I thought it was because of me.

My mother sent me away to an institution when I was six or seven. I felt my mother didn't want me because I was deaf. That was not the reason. Mother had a hard time taking care of me because I was so wild. She thought it was best for me to go to the institution to learn to associate with other deaf children. But I was very upset. I did not like sleeping at the school. I was scared. I thought my mother didn't love me because I'm deaf.

The teacher tried to calm me down. She told me I would learn with the other children. They were all talking sign language—talking with their hands. I didn't understand what they meant. I was confused, and I watched and watched. Slowly I understood. I knew nothing about deafness. I didn't know what it meant.

Finally after about five weeks, I got used to it.

I went to PSD* until I graduated. As I grew up, I understood more and more as to why I had to stay at the institution. But I begged and begged my mother many times to let me become a day student. I thought the school was like a prison: time to sleep, time to go, time for everything. I got fed up with it. But it's better to live in school. You learn more. You learn with each other and how to socialize with other children. I think that's best for them.

Communication

My mother learned some sign language. She has a book and I try to teach her. We communicate most of the time by lip-reading. I think parents should learn sign language. They should go to a school or college and learn. It's easier for the children to understand their parents. It's best to have both—lipreading and sign language.

When I was young, my relatives used signs with me and that embarrassed me. Now that I'm older, I understand there's nothing to be embarrassed about. People look at us using our hands. I would say, "Don't do that—lipread, lipread. It's less noticeable." That was when I was younger, though. Now I understand that I should not feel embarrassed. If people look, so what? Forget about people. Talk with people you wish and ignore other people around you. Before, I worried about people looking at me. But now, no more.

It's very embarrassing to have to write stuff. I never like writing. One time when a group of deaf were at a restaurant, a very mean waitress threw the paper and pencil at us. I became very angry and wanted to walk out, but the deaf people said, "Don't worry. Just write it down." I said, "No way." But the waitress had no patience with us. I was very tight because I don't like to write. I refused. I said, "Read my lips." I told her what I wanted and she was surprised.

Sometimes I have problems. When I meet strangers, I have

---

*Pennsylvania School for the Deaf

a hard time understanding them. If I know the people very well, there's no problem. If people ask me directions, I say, "I'm deaf. I lipread." Sometimes they walk away from me. Sometimes, depending on my mood, I'll just walk away.

I have friends, both deaf and hearing. I like hearing best. I like opposites—deaf and hearing. I feel I learn a lot. I feel more peaceful with hearing people. With the deaf, there's always trouble. They're always *against*. I have some friends that are deaf. Some. But I like to be with hearing people. That's me.

I *feel* like a hearing person because I work, I travel. I do many things like hearing people do. I have a TTY [teletypewriter] so I can use the phone. I always wished I could become hearing. It would be easier for me. I have problems with communication. Sometimes I become angry because I'm deaf. Not always.

Hearing aids

The teachers always forced me, *forced* me to wear a hearing aid. I was very stubborn about it. I never liked it. I did not feel good about it. It made me dizzy. They didn't believe me. I was constantly arguing with them about it. My mother was very angry and told the teachers to leave me alone. Oh, I hated the headphones we had to wear. They forced me—I must, I *must*, I MUST! I'd take them off. We'd have an argument. They'd put them back. They hurt my ears. Maybe I didn't understand why I was wearing them. That was when I was young.

I remember going to speech therapy and they said I should try wearing a hearing aid. When you go to a restaurant, or wherever, you can hear many things. But it didn't work out.

I can hear the water dripping. I can hear a bus. I hear everything but it makes me sick. It hurts my ears. It hurts down my throat. But the speech therapist said that's in my mind. She didn't believe me. I should learn to live in a noisy world—not a quiet world. Too much noise makes me nervous. I hear banging and I look all around trying to find the noise. It makes me disappointed because I want to hear everything.

Vocations

I trained in printing for four years. I wish I had taken hospital work, but PSD didn't have that kind of training. Now I am working in a hospital as a volunteer. I work in public relations and escort service. At lunch I feed the patients. I like that very much. But I'm disappointed there's no job opening yet. That would make my life. I get along fine in the hospital. I'm the only deaf one. Sometimes they have to write things, but most of the time I can get by, by lipreading. Some are very interested in learning signs. The patients like me very much. Every time I feed the patient, they kiss my hand and hold onto my hand. If they try to speak to me, I tell them that I'm deaf and they have to read my lips. I'm not ashamed or shy about saying, "I'm deaf."

I'm looking for a job. Over and over again. I'm constantly looking for jobs. Tomorrow I start at post office training in the mail machines. The letters go past and I put the numbers on. If I do very good, they'll give me a job. I don't know if I'll like it. For my life, I prefer movement.

I went to community college for training in computers. I understood what I was doing with the computers but I failed the test. It was the same test as for the hearing. I said, "It's not fair. It should be easier for the deaf." It was the vocabulary. It was very hard. So I dropped it. I was the only deaf person in the class. I had no patience.

For fun

I like photography. I like meeting famous people—people who are playing on TV. I like to meet them and take their pictures. I have a lot of pictures—Sophia Loren, Bette Davis. They come to Philadelphia for interviews, for shows. My friends that are deaf and I go and we meet them. I tell them, "I'm deaf. Can I take a picture with you?" They say, "okay." They put their arm around me. I figure if I tell them I'm deaf, they'll be nice to me and let me get my picture with them. That's me.

Eric's message. I would like people to be friendly and have happy faces. It's very important for hearing people to use facial expressions so the deaf can understand. Try to be patient with the deaf. Please don't give up on the deaf.

MARGIE (A Secretary)

Margie is a secretary for a deaf senior citizens' organiza-
tion. Although her parents are hearing people and she has
hearing brothers and sisters, Margie has a deaf brother and a
deaf sister. Her own children are hearing. A sign language
interpreter was used for the interview.

I had a deaf brother and a deaf sister. My deaf brother was
15 years older than myself. When he found out I was deaf, he
took me under his wing and taught me signs.* He started
teaching me when I was tiny—about two years old.

When I was in the high chair, my deaf brother always sat
with me. He would sit beside me and if I pointed, he would
smack my hand. He would say, "What?" I would sign—I
would make the sign for bread. If I just pointed, he would not
give it to me. The other people would be eating and talking,
eating and talking, and I would just kind of be watching and
signing with my brother. I began to realize that something was
wrong with me—I was different.

My mother and father could not sign because when my
brother was in school, the principal talked to my mother and
father and said, "*Don't* allow your children to sign. They *must*
learn to lipread." My mother would never use sign language
with me at all. I don't think that is a good idea. I was very
confused when I was small. I could never, *never* understand
my mother and father. I was shut off. They shut me off from
communication.

I went to the Pennsylvania School for the Deaf. I didn't like
it when I was little, but now I look back on it, I should be grateful. I lived at school and I didn't like it. Although I resented it
very much, very bitterly, it is really better to stay in school and
sleep in school. You get more benefits if you stay there—*if* you
are allowed to go home on weekends. Me, I was never allowed

---
*Sign language

to go home. I was allowed to go home for Christmas and summer vacation and that was all. That was the custom, that was the way it was done. It's better to stay in school on weekdays, go to class, play with other deaf children, circulate around, but on the weekends, you *need* your parents' love. You should be home with your family.

The classroom itself I liked very much, but when I finished the lesson and knew the lesson, I had to wait for all the other children to also know the lesson. That might have taken two weeks before we proceeded, and then I would understand and would have to wait for them to catch up to me again.

I enjoyed dormitory life. It was fun. I enjoyed being with other girls. Yeah, it was some fun, it really was. But still my favorite time was at home on the weekends. I didn't do anything at home. My mother had to work. She would come home tired on Friday; and Saturday and Sunday she would wash and iron and cook.

I am a senior aide for the Deaf Senior Citizens. I love it. *I love it.* Before, I worked in a lab for the electric company, soldering teeny little things. I worked with a microscope for nine years until my eyes became weak and I had to stop. I liked that job. I worked with hearing people. There were no deaf people. We played and teased each other. I had a great time. I could understand them or we wrote back and forth.

I like to do many, many things in my free time. Knitting. I just finished knitting a sweater. I like to make beaded flowers—beautiful flowers. I make dolls. I like to go to the deaf club where we have card games.

I am married, but we are separated. My husband is deaf. I have five children—they are all hearing. I don't sign with them. My husband did some signing so they know signs—most of them are homemade signs and a lot of fingerspelling. I talk orally to my children. I can discuss everything with them—we're a very close-knit family.

When strangers speak to me, I ask them to repeat because

I'm deaf. They'll explain to me and I'll talk to them. They seem to understand me. It doesn't bother me to tell people I'm deaf. I'm not ashamed of that.

I take advantage of being deaf sometimes

If I'm driving very quickly and a cop comes, I roll down the window and say, "What did I do?" The cop says, "You're driving too fast." "Who, me? I didn't know I was going that fast." He says, "Can you hear me?" I say, "No, I'm deaf." "Can you read my lips?" I answer, "Well, sort of." He says, "All right, all right," and he folds up the ticket and puts it in his pocket. "But go slow, be careful." In those times, I'm thankful to be deaf. It helps me out a lot.

HELEN (Retired)

Helen was born deaf. She relates a hospital experience.

I'll never forget that experience. It was terrible. I took my daughter shopping. We had a horrible car accident. We went to the hospital. I had broken my foot, and a Chinese doctor sent me to Xray. I went and they took a picture of my leg.

I said, "No, my foot. You can see my foot, it's broken." It curved at a strange angle.

The doctor said, "Nah, nah." He didn't pay attention to me.

"It's my foot. It's my foot."

He took a picture of my leg.

They gave me a bandage, but they didn't wrap my foot. You could see it was broken and swollen. I kept saying, "My foot. My foot."

They called in another doctor and he checked it out and did nothing.

I wasn't myself because of the accident. I was complaining and complaining for ten days in the hospital. They sent one doctor after another. All of the doctors paid attention to my leg, not my foot.

When I started to really come to, I looked around at the walls and noticed there was a note on the wall above my bed. I didn't have my glasses there so I really couldn't see it. My son, Jim, came and I asked him what the note on the wall said.

Jim said, "Now don't get mad."

I said, "What? Tell me!"

He said, "The people in the hospital think you're crazy."

"Why?"

"Because you've been signing and you have a funny voice, a strange voice, and you've been gesturing a lot."

Jim got the nurse and grabbed her and said, "That's my mother. She's deaf. She can read your lips. What did you write that on the wall for?"

But the doctor never tried to talk to me. The doctor sent me home. After I stayed in the hospital for ten days, the doctor sent me home. Home? I couldn't walk, but he said to go home. They ignored me.

So there I was at home. I couldn't walk. Jim took me to a podiatrist. We went in and explained it to the doctor. He looked and he didn't even need an Xray. He said, "It's broken."

They took me to the hospital. The same hospital. They put my foot under and Xrayed it. The doctor told me I would have to go to another hospital for an operation.

After the operation, the doctor said that if I had waited one more week, my foot would have had to be amputated because of blood vessel damage.

And that's the way they treated me because I was deaf. The doctors said they couldn't talk to me because I was deaf.

So I went to a lawyer and talked to him for two and a half hours. Funny thing, the lawyer had no trouble understanding me!

HARD
OF HEARING

BETTY
(A Coordinator
of Deaf Senior Citizens)

*Betty, in her fifties, has been hard of hearing since birth.
She has her dream job which is being coordinator of a deaf
senior citizens group.*

I have been hard of hearing since birth. Mother noticed right
after I was born that whenever she came in the room I didn't
stop crying until I saw her. The doctor wouldn't admit I was
hard of hearing until I was two years old. Mother always talked
in my ear and I'd say, "What'd you say, mother, what'd you
say?" I didn't want to miss anything.

At that time they didn't know what to do with a hard of
hearing child. She did the best she could. When she talked into
my ear she found that I could hear. She would go out in the
daytime and get all the gossip and all the news and bring it
back home and tell me. I had to learn at an early age not to
repeat what she told me. She figured since I didn't hear what
people were saying, that I wouldn't have any idea of what life
was like. She wanted to train me to know that people had
skeletons in the closet in order to give me an idea of what life
was like so when I grew up, I wouldn't be shocked or hurt.

I have no brothers or sisters. My mother said I had a
handicap so she didn't want to have other children. I don't
know my father's reaction, really. He always said that I would
hear one day. He believed that up until the last week before he
died. He had that faith.

They took me to various doctors. They tried those old-fashioned hearing aids. I couldn't hear with any of them. The first one was one of those carbon types. Everything sounded like Donald Duck. Quack, quack, quack, quack. I couldn't stand them.

It would have been helpful if they had learned sign language

Parents should keep talking to the child and try to keep their attention. Help them learn to read lips. Parents should learn sign language. I feel kids learn faster with sign language. I met one woman whose daughter is married now. She cannot nor has she ever been able to hold a conversation with her daughter. She has never known what her daughter feels. She wishes she had learned sign language and she said she's too old to learn now. But I think you're never too old to get a smattering of it, anyway. At that time it wasn't approved, so I never gave a thought to my parents learning sign language. It would have been helpful.

Hey, deafy!

I was sort of sheltered up to the time I went to school. When I got to school age, kids came to me and said in my ear, "Hey, deafy! Hi, deafy! Oooo, deaf." My mother went out on the porch, looked at them, and said, "I want everyone of you to go home and get on your knees tonight before you go to bed and thank the Lord for your hearing." From that time on, I never heard another thing from them. They were very helpful after that time. They were thankful they could hear.

Many, many times I was in the background, lonesome. I missed all the stories. I missed everything. I had close friends, but they were too busy when they were with a group. When there were three, I was alone. When there were two, I was involved. Just one to one. My mother always said, "Two's company, three's a crowd." That was the way she sort of brushed it off.

I went to a hearing school

I went to a hearing school. I had lipreading every Friday. I had speech training every day. I had my s's, my sh's, my ch's, my t's, and a lot of the sounds corrected. Years later, I met the principal of the school, and he said, "I'm glad I took you in. We learned a lot from you. It was quite an experience." I don't know what he meant, he didn't explain it, but he must have learned how to handle the hard of hearing and understood deafness better. It's possible.

I always sat up front. The teacher sat or stood near me. I could hear a little bit and read lips along with it which helped. I had one teacher in high school I'll never forget. Every time she gave a spelling test, she'd walk around the room. After the third test, she said, "Betty, what's wrong with you? Don't you know your spelling?" I said, "You walk around the room and by the time I get what you say on your lips and write it down, you're not on the next one, but the following one." And I said, "Besides, I'm not a giraffe to follow you around the room like that." She said, "Sit down." And she went through every word and I got 100 percent.

The teachers would send homework home, and I would work with my mother. I was a bad girl then. I was having a hard time with a test in chemistry and two of the girls would come to my house every night to tutor me. All the girls were lipreading the answers during the test. The teacher caught them and put me in another room and gave me the tests.

I was very popular with boys until I got to about 13. I think I was extremely shy. The boys talked to me, but I didn't understand a word they said. I'd get so nervous, I couldn't understand them. I had been used to talking to boys, but then I became more self-conscious about my deafness.

Are you glad you went to hearing school?

Yes and no. I see that the deaf have a closer relationship than I'll ever be able to get. When you grow up at school, you form close relationships with your classmates. You have that feeling of closeness; you talk about the good old days. When you're coming to the deaf community later in life, you don't have that certain something that they have.

Mother tried to get me into the school for the deaf. The principal wouldn't take me. He said in six months I would lose my voice. I don't know whether I would have had clear speech or whether I would have developed as much as I did if I'd gone to the school for the deaf. Maybe I would have learned more. I don't know.

My best age was when I got involved with the hard of hearing. After I finished school, they invited me. They wanted to start a group for hard of hearing young adults. I became very active in that. Those were the happiest days of my life. I met others like myself. I formed some very, very close friendships during that period.

Communication

Hearing aids are not perfect, you know. You still miss a lot of conversation. You feel like you're the only one in the room, all by yourself. In school, they would start talking and I'd get tired of trying to hear them. So I walked around the auditorium. Finally a black girl said, "Come on over here and sit with us." They talked to me and made me feel at home.

People could help me by giving me a rundown of what is happening; by not letting me get suspicious of what was said. Sometimes when you're deaf, you can misinterpret very easily what they're saying, and you feel they're talking against you. If they keep me posted what they're talking about, I can follow. I hate speakers with mustaches or beards—that distracts from the lips.

The people that are most understanding are the ones that have had deafness in the family or friends that were deaf. I had a cousin that used to introduce me as his hard of hearing cousin. When you get introduced to a person that way you feel a wall going up between you and the other person. No matter what you say to that person, you cannot break through that wall. Always better to let the hard of hearing person establish contact with the other person. If the hard of hearing person wants to tell the hearing person that she is hard of hearing, fine. By that time, you've made a contact. If you're introduced as hard of hearing, they sort of freeze. They look uncomfortable. They're scared, scared to death of you. You can see it in their eyes. They're scared of communicating with you.

My dream job is the job I've had for the past eight years—working with the deaf and hearing-impaired senior citizens. This has been my happiest time. I feel I am involved. I don't feel left out.

I remember when I was a teenager, I was all upset by my deafness and wondering why I was deaf. My mother said, "The Lord works in mysterious ways. He might be preparing you for something great. You might be able to work with the deaf or hearing impaired. You never know." I accepted that. When I was 50 years old, I started to do what the Lord prepared for me.

Betty's message. Make sure the hard of hearing person is not an outsider. Include them. Bring them up to date once in a while. I've had friends who are very kind and stop conversations to tell me what was said, then [they] go on.

ELIZABETH (A Volunteer)

People we see with walkers, hearing aids, canes, and gray hair are labeled the "elderly." Elizabeth helps us to personalize this group by telling how it feels to be over 70. She has recently started to wear a hearing aid.

My husband worked for the city of Philadelphia. He passed away ten years this December. I live alone in my own home. I get Social Security and then there's survivor pension. He worked for the city for 42 years.

I volunteer

I do volunteer work twice a week up at CLA [community living arrangements]. I've been going for nine or ten years. I'm in with the lunch program. We set tables and prepare for all the people coming in. They have about 100 every day for lunch. I like it very much. I like it because you meet a lot of nice people, and they're friendly. I think it helps a lot of others just by talking to them.

I enjoy it if I'm helping somebody or doing something for somebody else, which I do a lot. Besides working two days a week as a volunteer, I go to three other people every day of the week. I pay their gas bills, I get their checks cashed, I get their medicine. The woman who lives next to me is 83. There's another woman down the street who must be close to 90. I pay bills for her. I get her anything she wants from the Acme. I get newspapers. They're neighbors who've been there for a number of years.

I never feel lonely. Even when I'm home, I'm never lonely. I'm a person that prays a lot and I feel that if you have belief in God, you're not lonely.

Some lose their patience

I've noticed my hearing problem about three years, but gradually it's getting worse. When you get out with people, they get tired of talking to you when they have to speak loud. Some lose their patience. If you're in a crowd, they'll say, "Oh, she can't hear." You're just sort of isolated. Some people are impatient. A lot of times I have to ask people to repeat. It depends on people's voices. Some people's voices carry more than others. Some people repeat. Others say, "Forget it." I think if a hearing aid will help me, it's very nice.

I guess with my age, I'm "elderly." I know some elderly people that are younger than me, that aren't as active as I am. I don't feel as if I am really elderly yet. Maybe I need a cane [laughs].

Elizabeth's message. Always trust and love God and you have nothing to worry about. God is your creator and he's the one who's going to take care of you. He said, "I'll be with you always."

5. SIGHT
All's Clear, C'mon!

I like to be asked if people can help. I like to be conversed with. A lot of people waiting for the bus don't just stand there looking at each other—they converse. Include me in it. I appreciate asking if you can help me across the street. And, "How about taking my arm and we'll cross the street together.
                    —Lucy

So what if I'm blind,
I really don't mind,
This is not a sympathy plea.

But when I'm around
You act like a clown—
The problem is you, not me.
                    —Jack McCloskey

 # BLIND AND PARTIALLY SIGHTED

Blindness is almost incomprehensible to those of us who can see. How do the blind get along in everyday life? How much can they see? How much help do they need and want? What is the best schooling that can be provided for adjustment to a sighted world? Although a diversity of opinion is presented, there will be insights. One comes from Lucy: "The one thing that bothers me most in the whole world is being treated as if we are different because we are handicapped. We are different because we are different individuals. I feel like an individual."

There are those who are defined as legally blind (to see at twenty feet what a normally sighted person would see at 200 feet) but who are actually partially sighted. They may have enough sight to use corrective lenses or a telescopic lens. Although a telescopic lens makes it possible to see at greater distances, and may even enable a partially sighted person to read, the social stigma of wearing an apparatus so unusual may preclude its use.

Albinism is lack of pigment in the skin, eyes, and hair. Because of the lack of pigment in the eyes, albinos are partially sighted. Although people with albinism were asked for interviews based on their cosmetic differences, it soon became apparent that the cosmetic problem was secondary to the sight problem.

With one voice, the blind and partially sighted people interviewed for this book affirmed, "I may be blind or partially sighted, but that's something separate—that's not *me*."

BLIND

GEORGE
(A Vocational Rehabilitation Counselor)

George was a high school dropout. He was sighted until he was eighteen years old. As a result of a hunting accident, he lost his sight. He went to Overbrook School for the Blind in Philadelphia and then to college. He is now a rehabilitation counselor at the Office for the Visually Handicapped. When I walked into the office, a coworker was helping him by describing the contents of a package left on his desk. George checked his braille watch, and discovered it was time for our appointment.

I have light perception in the right eye, which doesn't mean a thing. I can look up and maybe I can catch a glimmer of light, but I can't use that light to get around. The left eye is artificial. Most people have some type of light perception. There are very few totally blind people in the world.

I became blind through an accident a long time ago. In 1948 I was involved in a hunting accident—small game hunting. I was eighteen. I've been blind now for 33 years.

I remember when I first learned that I was going to be blind—permanently. After seventeen days in the hospital, I had gone to visit neighbors in the next room. The family doctor came and I'm sitting in a chair visiting, and I'm feeling pretty good about things, not knowing the outcome really. I sort of suspected. When I was struck by the pellets from the shotgun blast, there was no pain. One pellet hit this bone here and went behind the right eye and took off the optic nerve. I knew my eyes were hit and that was it. I didn't see a thing from that second on. And yet they kept working on the one eye—they were trying to save the left eye. And when the doctor walked in, all he said was, "Well, George, you'd better think of higher education." Then he turned and walked out. And, boy, I tell you, I felt like the bottom line was that I was blind—and that I was going to stay blind.

I wanted to be independent

From then on I wanted to be independent. I wanted to prove that I'm not going to be dependent on anybody. And if anybody said, "You're not going to do something," that's when I said, "I'm going to do it." Maybe it was good and maybe it wasn't always.

I think it was my first year after the accident when I decided that I was going to do something one of my brothers was asked to—it was to put on a screen door. I went out to the barn, got the door, carried it in, and I hung it. Seems from that point my dad began to realize, "Hey, maybe he will be able to do something."

I told my mother one day after I got home from the hospital that I was going to walk into town. She said, "You are?" And I had to walk a mile and a half to two miles. I started out and I said to myself, I know exactly where I am. I can *feel* where I am. I crossed the turnpike bridge. I followed the road and came to the macadam. I followed the edge of the road all the way into town. I just had a cane hanging on my arm. I said, "My, this is easy." I found the drugstore I was going to. Years later I found out what my mother did. Two of my brothers tagged after me. But you know what? They followed me halfway and they went home. They said, "He's doing fine. He doesn't need us."

I was eighteen. That happened in November 1948. By the next year, September, I left home and came here to

Philadelphia to pursue an education. I was faced with the ultimate blindness and it was suggested that I better get further training. My family brought me to Overbrook School for the Blind so I could finish high school.

I tend toward mainstreaming

I tend to lean toward mainstreaming because I think the intelligent handicapped student is going to get a better deal in life. They'll have a better understanding of their handicap. They'll know right from the beginning how they're going to deal with the so-called normal world.

I just feel that we've come to an age and a time in life where we're trying to open doors in industry and employment and hire the handicapped. So the public might as well get used to having handicapped people around. Why shut them off into a separate place?

The problem in my case was that I was nineteen years old. I certainly wasn't going to get back into the regular school. I needed time to adjust to my blindness, so I needed Overbrook. They gave me an opportunity I didn't expect. They allowed me to stay there for five years. I didn't enter the University of Pennsylvania until age 24. At age 24 I was ready for college. It took me all that time to learn braille, to get through all my four years of high school. So Overbrook, in that sense, was good for me.

Would you have chosen the same vocation if you had not been blinded?

When I was sitting in that hat factory, before I became blind, and I was feeding felt hats into a machine, I was always wondering, "Now, what am I going to do?" I was thinking maybe of getting into some kind of business. I know I'd never have finished high school, four years of the university, and some graduate work at Temple. That wouldn't have been my choice. I know that.

We're a state agency here. I came and worked for ten years

for what I had originally been trained to do—and that's to go out into the homes and help people grab a hold of their blindness. In the back of my mind I thought I might like to try vocational rehabilitation counseling some day. In 1977 that opportunity came and I took it. I have no desire to do anything else right now. I really like working with people. I like getting out there. I can plan my day as I feel, and I like it. At age 51, I'm not looking for too many new things to do.

This place is not set up for blind people. My job can only get done through my own efforts. I must use volunteer people—and I use lots of them. That's the only way I can get my reading done. Sometimes it's the only way I can get reports typed. As far as getting to know my people, contacting them, and going out and seeing them, visiting employers, doing anything like that—I can do that. I don't need anyone. But when it's filling out a form, specifically, I don't have any specialized equipment available to me. I'm only successful by my own efforts.

At 51, I'm getting tired of hassling. In the next ten, fifteen years I still hope to be productive, but can't it be done a little easier? I wish I had six hours of secretarial help. I have learned to organize things. My co-workers always remark to me how well organized I am. But they don't know I have to be if I'm going to get along and do my job. We can say to one of our colleagues, "What's this?" or "What's that?" if you don't have a reader at the moment. But you can't draw on them to sit for any length of time.

Do you ever feel like a second-class citizen?

It may be true with other handicapped people. I feel sometimes it comes from the handicapped persons themselves—something they haven't come to grips with. They allowed themselves to take a second-class citizen position, perhaps. There are blind out on the street today who'd rather hold a tin cup.

The only times I feel in some ways what you're saying . . . when I see two other men that I meet on the train and they might be more easy with each other. When they're with me they're a little more cautious. Maybe it's a feeling of not knowing what to say. Maybe a little bit of that is there—I'm still a blind man. Basically, I don't think it is that much of a problem.

Do you appreciate having people come up to you and ask if you need help?

People do ask me. A good many don't. It all depends. They want to help, but they're not sure how. I don't turn it down because maybe the next fellow might need it more. I hate it when blind people treat the public in such a way that it wants to turn them off. You never know when you might need it. If people offer, sure. It gives me another chance to say "hello" to another personality and get to know a little bit about them, exchange a few words. They might grab you and sort of lift you instead of lead you, but you can maneuver out of that situation and get into a more comfortable position.

If you need help, what do you do?

I just stand and hope. If you look forlorn enough, somebody might come and help you. You get stuck in an area where there's just nobody around and you need some information. That's the worst. I knock on lots of doors until I rouse somebody and I say, "Hey, I'm looking for so and so. Where am I?" On one of the cold, cold windy days we had this last month, getting across 36th and Market—the traffic is atrocious in the first place—I was sure glad when I heard a voice that said, "All's clear. C'mon."

How does your wife adjust to your blindness?

My wife helps me out. We've been married 28 years. It's just a natural guiding kind of thing where she places my hand and says, "The chair's here." She can drop me off at the men's room. I always have my cane anyway. She'll meet me at the door later.

I just don't go to movies that much. My son goes with her. I fall asleep. Occasionally I hit a good movie that I like. It's got to be a good story, some good talking. But if there's a lot of action—"What's going on up there?" I love to go to plays. We go to dinner shows a lot. She and I work it out. I can get in the line with her and get my food. She helps me.

My wife and I have no problems. She does resent my cane. I've never asked her point-blank about it. But she doesn't want the cane to be in evidence when I'm out. And I don't know why that is. Maybe because she's with a blind man and that makes people look. I don't know if that's it or, sometimes if a person is with a blind person, then they are also associated as being blind. It might be that. I really don't know. But she says, "You don't need that thing out." All right. I don't keep it out. I tuck it away. I get mad. It irks me.

How do your children react?

They're 28, 25, and 21 now. They didn't know me any other way than being blind. If only the general public could react the way my own sons did ... when they were babies and I was changing their diapers, and they couldn't even talk, I laid a diaper pin down and I'm looking for it—*all* of them with their own little hand would pick the pin up and put it in my hand. That happened with the first one, and I thought, "Isn't that something!" But when it happened with all three of them...! I guess they said, "Well, c'mon, pop, let's get this over with." The little hand would just put the pin right in my hand. As they went on through life, they began to learn very quickly that daddy has to feel and mother has to see things. They would always hold things up for her, but they would put my hand on the page or the picture.

One day I was in the kitchen doing dishes. Kevin, the oldest—he was 11 or 12—said, "I want you to see this, dad." "Well, my hands are wet." I dried my hands and I said, "I'm ready to look at it." "Oh, I showed it to you already." "What do you mean?" "I put it against your *leg*." I chased him out the front door right away. "Get out of here!"

They were always bringing kids home, not to say they had a blind dad, but, "Pop, show them how you can identify money when it hits the floor—quarters, nickels, dimes." I never had my braille watch. It was always off to school, showing it to somebody.

You have excellent eye contact

Absolutely, because I was sighted. Sometimes I'm not sure of the eye contact. Sometimes I might be looking too far to the right. You learn facial contacts by seeing. I saw for eighteen years. Anyone who was born blind has to work very hard on it. I used to tell the kids at Overbrook who were blind, "Look at me. I'm over here. Look at me when you talk." It has to be stressed. It has to be emphasized. I try to be conscious of that. I don't guess that I'll ever lose it.

I get asked whether it's different than being blind at birth. I guess everybody could answer that differently. I appreciate the fact that I saw for eighteen years. I can tell you what everything looks like. I know the moon up in the sky. I've seen all that for eighteen years. In my case I am glad that I had vision for that length of time. But you may talk to someone who was born blind and they may feel, "What you've never seen, how do you know what you're missing?"

Did your blindness change your personality?

Basically, I always liked people. That has never changed. I still love to be around people. I still like to be the center of attraction sometimes. I like to kid around. That hasn't changed. I like to make people laugh.

Do you blame anyone for your blindness?

If you want me to get philosophical, I can do that. There was a blind man in my town. Every time I walked past his home, prior to my accident, I would close my eyes and practice walking. Then I'd shudder and say, "I'm going to be blind." And then I'd shake the thing out of my mind. "That's stupid." That happened several times. I thought it was coincidence.

In October, that same year as my accident, I looked toward the setting sun and saw the prettiest sight I can remember. I can still see it now—the redness of the sun. I couldn't see the sun directly but saw all the redness on the cloud. Just the way the sun set—the blues and the whites—oh! It was just the most *gorgeous* thing. I again had that feeling: "You're never going to see that again." And a few days later, strange as it may seem, I had the accident.

I was maybe more religious than I am now. When I lost my sight I did a lot of praying—for strength, courage, and faith. I think I got it. That's all I ever asked for. I never asked for anything else. I think that helped me.

There's only a very few times I wish I could see. Then I wouldn't have to depend on somebody. A blind person might as well forget going to a supermarket. You *can't* do it. When they took away clerks and put in self-service, that's when they messed the whole thing up. I could never paint the house, but I always substituted. I took over many of the chores my wife would normally have done. I do the laundry, the dishes, I always bathed the kids. I scrub the floor. All of that stuff. We traded off.

Is your church sensitive to you?

Oh, yes. No problems. I make them. I *make* people react to me. Maybe I'm an egotistical so and so. But I just like to be with people. I pitch in and do whatever. I always get stuck with the dishes at the pancake breakfast. I'm stereotyped that way. At least George can do the dishes. I accept my role. I do my dishes for four hours whenever we have a pancake breakfast. That's fine. I'm not the only guy doing dishes. I've been on committees. I function in other ways. Sometimes they don't realize what I can do. They want to be overly helpful to me at times. I say, "What are you going to do while I'm out going to work on Monday? You going to come along, hold my hand while I'm running around Philadelphia or Delaware County?"

Do you ever have fear?

Lots of fear, yes. I'm a big sissy. Only with the unknown. What I hear and can't see or identify, yeah. I'm afraid of mice [laughs]. I hate the little buggers.

I'm not afraid to go anywhere. I used to think, "What if I get mugged?" It happened to me once in Philadelphia. They were just little kids and they tricked me into going down an alley and took my money. I said, "C'mon, you guys, you don't want this stuff." I knew they were little kids. I wasn't terribly afraid, but it made me edgy going back into that neighborhood for a while.

We go camping. I go all over the campground by myself. Now there are people who *admire* me for doing it and I'll hear people, "Well, he's foolhardy, walking all over the campground." Sometimes I think they think I'm crazy and that I'm not blind. I heard that already, too. Well, he's a fake. He can see. When I did door-to-door selling, I would go out, knock on doors all by myself. I had people call the cops—"There's a fake out here." I didn't carry my cane. Tell me what you want a blind man to look like and I'll do it—if that's what they want.

If you had three wishes?

You want me to say, get your sight back [laughs]. It really isn't. If it came back, after 33 years of blindness, I wouldn't know my family in a crowd of ten to twelve people. I don't know if I could pick them out unless they smiled. Three wishes—to see my grandson or the new one that's coming. If I were going to be practical, one wish would be to clear up our debts. I want financial security like everyone else. I would wish for peace in the world.

Is there anything you wish you could do?

The only time I'd say is when I feel totally dependent. Suppose my wife were to die. We have always been together doing things. I had my family and I learned through them and saw through them. If all of a sudden I had to go to Atlantic City all by myself, today, I'd almost tell you to forget about it. What would I do? Sure, when I go to the shore, I explore. And I go out on my own. But to go somewhere completely by myself, forget it! I don't want to ever be alone.

I consider myself a well-adjusted blind person who has accepted what I am. Yet, I'm not different than many, many hundreds of other people. I don't feel unique. And I don't think I should.

LUCY
(A Receptionist and Teacher)

She fixed a cup of freshly brewed coffee and pastry in the kitchen. She had forgotten to put on the lights for me and the preparations were made in the dark. Then she made me comfortable, arranged the lights in the living room, sat on the edge of her chair, and prepared to answer my questions. Lucy is 63 years old, dark-haired, slim, and vivacious. Her home is neat as a pin, beautifully decorated with a collection of owls, all arranged and dusted. She is a receptionist at the Overbrook School for the Blind in Philadelphia.

I explained the purpose of the book . . .

I know exactly what you're talking about because the one thing that bothers me most is being treated as if we are different because we are handicapped. We are different because we are different individuals. I feel like an individual.

I *am* treated differently in a group. If I'm invited out, the very first thing that happens is, I'm not allowed to do anything. If I'm in someone else's home, I'm the kind of person who'll insist on knowing where I am. But if I'm out in a reception area or a large place, I'm sat at one place and somebody comes and says, "Hi, Lucy. How are you, Lucy?" But to be able to mill around, I just can't do it because . . . I'm different than they. They almost speak to me as if I am different. I mean, you can hear it in their voices. You are not part of them. It's true. It's a strain. You're going out for a good time, but it's a strain. But you can really get through it because you can make them accept you.

I do need help, for instance, to go to a ladies' room in a strange place. So immediately I'm different because I'm holding your arm and I'm going where you're taking me. It should be very nicely said. If I say, "Let's go to the ladies' room," and Carol says, "Well, c'mon, Lou, let's go." You know what I mean. Not, "No, wait a minute. Now Lucy's going to the ladies' room. I've got to take her to the ladies' room." It really can be done. It's just that people don't know how.

It's such a hard thing. Maybe I can explain it if I give you examples. I was walking to work one day; and instead of saying "Good morning" to me as I went by, my neighbors waited until I went seven or eight houses past them. Thinking I couldn't hear as well as not being able to see, they said, "Boy, doesn't she look nice going to work every day?" So you know, I couldn't help it. I turned around and walked back and said, "You know, Mary, that would have been very nice if you'd said that to me so that I could appreciate it and thank you rather than wait until I got miles away." What it did to me was make me nervous. And in my walking, I almost stumbled over one of the rock gardens.

Were you born without sight?
The cause of my blindness was too much silver nitrate at birth. When I was eighteen months old, my dad came home from work one day and threw a penny on the floor. He discovered that instead of me going right for it, my hands went around it. He immediately got in touch with our doctor and took me to Wills Eye Hospital to do everything possible they absolutely could. When the family knew there was going to be total blindness, the first thing they did was treat me like the rest of the family—which I am very, very grateful for.

I would go to a residential school any day
I'm glad I went to Overbrook School for the Blind. I got the proper education. I wouldn't have appreciated going to a sighted school.

[She tells of a brother who had a tumor and fell down on his way home from school. The kids made fun of him. She knew even then that she did not want to have other kids make fun of her for her blindness.]

I used to say to myself, "Thank God I'm going to Overbrook!" Rather than having to face blindness *and* struggle to go to school, I would go to a residential school any day. I was ready for my blindness when I got out of school. Now I think when you reach high school, that if you have the ability because you have already gotten your foundation, I have nothing against your going to a regular day school. But I still say, if you can take *all* of your training in residential [school] and then go to college, you can stand up to the rest of it.

Is there something wrong with me?

I used to read a print book, as if I was really reading. Not that I resented my braille, because I love my braille. But my sister tells me now the many times she used to catch me, sitting in my bedroom with a book and I'd move my head side to side from one side of the page to the other side. I never knew she saw me do this.

My most difficult age was when I first came home from school—I mean when I graduated. One may be very content to listen to the radio, read books, do whatever one was going to do, constantly. Well, I wasn't. When I was between the years of 21 and 25, I would be so annoyed and say to myself, "Why am I any different? Why can't I be out with other people?"

Anyway, they were my frustrating years. I used to see my girlfriends go out with their boyfriends. I literally used to shed tears. When my family would be out and maybe I would be baby-sitting, I would say, "Why?" I really did.

My very first job was working for the Commission for the Blind in New Jersey. They had a little workshop set up in my area of Trenton. I used to go in and sew bias binding on aprons, like coverall aprons, and little, tiny, fancy aprons. And with earning my own living, I paid for my own telephone because my family couldn't afford one. That way I could get in touch with my friends.

As I got older, I didn't think that was quite what I wanted. Then I went out to work. I enjoyed myself very much and made a lot of friends. And, of course, to me I was going to work just like the outside world. This meant a lot to me.

I like to be conversed with

I like to be asked if people can help. I appreciate asking if you can help me across the street. And, "How about taking my arm and we'll cross the street together?" I like to be conversed with. A lot of people waiting for the bus don't just stand there looking at each other—they converse. Include me in it.

Going into stores is kind of a hard thing, although I've done it. Because the stores are so crowded there isn't much movement a blind person can do. Your cane is going to help you out of the way of things that are in the area of the length of your cane, but it's not going to help you not brush things off the counter. There's no excuse why we can't go shopping because we can make arrangements with managers and floor walkers.

The whole drawback is on the other person wondering what you want. Blind people are partly to blame because we have some that will shun and they don't want to be bothered *at all*. I resent that because it's making it bad for me.

The same way when I'm out eating. If I really want something, I'll order it. My friends know me well enough that they'll say, "How about me cutting that?" and switch plates. In the beginning, I used to refuse. I used to say, "No, no, no," and either I would just nibble at it or never eat it. Like the first time John ever took me out. He was partially sighted himself. I ordered a vegetable platter. He said, "You don't want that." I said, "Yes, I do." Well, I ate hardly any of it because I was ashamed at the time to say I couldn't handle it. But, boy, I soon learned.

Lucy's message. Thank me for what I do. Congratulate me for what is necessary, but don't constantly come to me and say I'm great, I'm this, I'm that. Because I simply can not stand it. "Oh she's wonderful." "You should see her home." I can't tell them to stop this praising bit—you know what I mean? Where do I touch it?

I want *anybody* to tell me I have a spot on my clothes because if I knew that I went around all day looking obnoxious, then that would bother me more than anybody telling me about it.

We can't read a newspaper, but we can still talk about the news. We listen to the news on the radio.

Let me tell you something I'm missing. They're getting more and more on TV where they're not explaining the way they used to explain. When I first started listening to the string bands, I mean the explanations of their outfits were so great. Now they're describing them less and less. I *love* Miss America. I just *love* to know what they're wearing. One year, you'll get hardly any explanation; the next year, you'll get a beautiful explanation. With sports, for instance, John would always have the TV on, but the radio for me because the radio has to give more explanation than TV does. But there's no reason the TV can't [be more descriptive] whether there's a picture or not. They're there anyway.

There was a commercial that was very interesting to me. It was an article—a household article—that I really would have wanted to send for. But then they said, "This is available in these stores. . . ." *and not one sound.* So where do you go?

My biggest wish is that there was a way to teach blind people to laugh and smile normally—if there was only a way. But there is no way for the simple reason that we cannot see what the next person is doing.

I would love to see my flowers. Now I see them with my hands, and I know my plants and they're beautiful to me, but I'd love to see them.

What fascinates me the most: I do not like snow as snow, but when others look out the window after a first snow and tell me how *gorgeous* it is, I imagine it in my own mind, but I know it's not the right picture. I know it can't be the same as theirs and this is what I would like to experience.

JERRY
(A Vocational Rehabilitation Counselor)

Jerry, blind from the age of five, is a vocational counselor, serving visually impaired clients. He is in his early forties. He was married at one time to a sighted woman, but now lives alone in a Philadelphia high-rise. "My life has been a succession of proving myself," he says of himself.

When I grew up, I was a hoodlum. Oh, yeah, I was bad. I used to be the leader of a gang called the Royal Dukes. The only way you could be a member of that gang, you had to be the president or the warlord of another gang. So only presidents or warlords could be in it, and I was the leader of *that* group. We had gang wars. My reputation was such that people, if they were going to fight me, they would try to hit me and duck or get away from me. But I was exceptionally fast. I remember fighting this one guy—I didn't realize how big this guy was. I was shocked to realize how big he was, right? So I'm lookin' up and woofin' and then we started fighting. What I did was put my right arm around his waist and my left arm between his legs. Picked him up and drove him right into the concrete. His head hit the concrete, then I was on him and that was it.

The idea of confidence

I had glaucoma and lost my vision when I was five. The way they found out I had glaucoma is because I was having severe headaches. It wasn't the fact that I was aware my vision was lessening. I was in the hospital from four and a half to six and a half years old. They tried to save my vision and I had a series of operations. I spent so much time in the hospital they had to wean me away from my mother; and when it was time to go home, they had to start weaning me back to my mother.

One of the greatest things in my favor is that I come from a relatively large family. I have seven brothers, of which I'm the oldest. My father did a lot for me to make me independent. He would have me tying and untying my shoes, putting my clothes on properly, taking them off. When I started at the Maryland School for the Blind, I was helping the housemother dress and undress the sixteen- and seventeen-year-olds. Many of them came from a situation where they were more protected. They hadn't been allowed to dress themselves. I don't think that's as common now as it was in the forties. I think if it were left to my mother, I probably wouldn't be as independent because of the mother's instinct. I still have trouble with her wanting to oversee my life.

But my father wasn't like that. I got punished just like the rest of the kids. If they got a spanking, I got one. Another thing that helped me to be independent is the idea of confidence. My brothers looked up to me. Whatever I said pretty much was the thing. In a lot of instances blind members of a family are looked down on, rather than looked up to. This hurts their self-image. If you had the kind of support that I had then, you can't help but succeed.

I hate to be second best

I went to the Maryland School for the Blind until the tenth grade. Then I went to regular public school. The School for the Blind went up to the twelfth, but if you were going to be an academic student and go to college, they would transfer you out of the protective setting of a residential school to send you into a public school. I agree with this mode.

We had volunteer readers, kids who were in the surrounding colleges, who would come and read for us in the evening. There were three of us blind kids in high school. This was sort of an experiment because two of us were black. This was the first time they had ever done any integrating.

It was a noted high school and had some rather outstanding people come from there. The first two days I was there, I developed an extreme pain in my stomach and started vomiting blood. They took me to Johns Hopkins [Hospital]. What it amounted to was I was having a psychosomatic illness. That was my way of getting out of going. When it was found out there was really nothing wrong with me, I was all right.

My fear was that I wouldn't succeed, that I wouldn't be as bright [as others]. I hate to be second best. I felt that with all this talent around, I might not even be second best, but way down the line. But I was fortunate to graduate as an honor student.

I was an exceptionally good athlete, particularly in wrestling. When I came to high school, my reputation preceded me. Which helped. There were a number of guys on the wrestling team who knew about my record from the school paper, so to a degree, I had an advantage. I got acceptance and it built up my confidence in myself to the point that I even had to pull back sometimes because I was too aggressive.

[Jerry feels that attending a a school for the blind during the early years is advantageous.]

In Philadelphia they do a lot of mainstreaming. I feel that for the first and most crucial years it would be better for a blind person to be in a situation where he feels comfortable. In a residential school with everybody having the same or similar disability, you don't have to worry about being picked at or worrying about all of the attitudes. In the crucial years it would be better for individuals to be in a residential school until they really get a grasp in their education, have a strong base from which to build. If they plan to go to college, then I feel they should spend a number of years, preferably three or four years, in a regular public school setting. That way they will have a chance to deal with society the way they will have to deal with society from then on.

You get a transition from a residential situation to an extremely outgoing situation, as college is, by going through high school. Many of my classmates who started college with me bombed out the first semester because they thought it was the thirteenth year of high school.

I went to summer school before college and took two courses. That way I got to know the campus, the various classrooms, the buildings. I was oriented. I got to make some friends when the pressure wasn't on me. They introduced me to other folks. As a matter of fact, during the orientation period I was even telling people how to get to certain classes. That was an advantage. I used to walk across campus with my cane hanging in my coat and my hands in my pocket with my briefcase under my arm. People'd say, "He's not blind, the way he does that."

I ran into two types of attitudes from my professors. As a blind person, the fact you were able to get to college meant that whatever you did, you would be rewarded highly. I might have gotten an A or two that I didn't deserve. I had the other attitude from professors, that since you are able to get there, meant that you are a super person and you should do super work. So a couple of C's that I got might have been A's or B's. I guess it balanced out in the long run.

Forcing myself

I remember situations of forcing myself to do things that inside I was terribly afraid of. When this blind friend of mine and I would go into the cafeteria, he would sit at a table and wait until eventually somebody who knew us would say, "Can I help you?" A lot of times I would get up and walk to the line and say, "Excuse me, please, can you help me?" What bothered me more than anything was that folks were so taken aback they would stand there with their mouths open and wouldn't say a word. Then I'd just move farther down the line and somebody'd say, "Sure, I'll give you a hand." It was a traumatic experience, but I would force myself to do it. Then it started to become easier and people got to know me more. I made myself available to them.

My two brothers closest to my age and I used to hang out quite a bit. Whenever they were invited to affairs, they would have me come along. If folks didn't want me along, my brothers would say, "If you don't want him, we won't come." After people had some dealing with me, they found I wasn't any different from them.

Toward the end of my freshman year was a really tough time. I really love the ladies, right. I talked, rapped to various girls and they thought it was great. But when we had affairs where the girls would invite the guys, it wasn't that often I was invited even by the same ones that were talking the good talk to me. That was rather traumatic.

But I just kept plugging away at it and eventually I did make some worthwhile contact. They didn't have to try to make friends with me because I made friends with them. I was outgoing and aggressive. After a while it got to the point where they thought I was just one of the guys.

Everything got silent

I'm not always comfortable, even now, in an extremely new setting. When I went to graduate school and walked into the classroom, everybody was blabbing to each other. I walked in the door and, just like that, everything got silent. That shook me up. I knew all eyes were on me to see whether I could find the chair. When I found the chair—and nobody offered to help me—and sat down, it started buzzing again and everything was back to normal. The most important thing is that when I walk into a room, I like everyone to continue what they're doing even if they're watching me outta the corner of their eye. That way, I get the impression they're not watching me, even if they are.

If I go to a place once and make a supreme effort to know the place, then all I need is that one time. No one likes to show the rough edges of a situation very often. If I make a mistake and people see me, they say, "Oh, isn't it a shame?" and rush to help me. The subway system was really a traumatic situation the first few times with the trains making a lot of noise. *Noise to a blind person is like fog to a sighted person.*

It bothers me if I'm in a restaurant and the waitress will

come up and say, "What does he want?" I've always asked any person that I'm with to not say anything or refer the person to me. Usually I'll say, "What he really would like to have is . . . ." They say, "Oh!" The next time they come around, they'll say, "Excuse me, sir, what would you like?" Because you make a joke of it rather than being sharp with them, they come around. You take the burden of responsibility off the persons that you're dealing with and place it on yourself, then it makes it easier for them to adjust, to accept.

One time I was out in the rain and this guy was heading home from the store. I told him where I would like to go, and he said, "Man, you're really way off the trail." He started giving me directions and then he said, "Oh, well, I'm not doing anything, come on. I'll walk you." Then he said, "I'll stand until you are accepted inside to determine whether this is the right place or not." Basically, I can honestly say that I've been extremely fortunate.

I'm mellowing out

Most of my close friends are sighted, but I'm mellowing out. One time I don't think I would have even gone with a blind girl. Not so much because I didn't find a blind girl attractive, but because of the type of person I am. I want to be number one. Having a sighted girl would take more of an effort to win her favor than winning another blind person's favor, but I'm mellowing out. I still lean that way, but I'm not so strung out that if I came across a really together lady I would say because of this I would not go out.

On the job

I'm a vocational rehabilitation counselor. The job responsibilities are basically dealing with visually disabled individuals and guiding them through a pre-vocation, vocational, and, hopefully, a placement situation. I've been fortunate because I can relate to a number of my clients because I grew up in the ghetto. Most of my clients are black. We like to say our greatest responsibility is counseling and guidance and placement. A lot of it is getting an individual to a point where he feels confident enough to be able to do what it is that will eventually lead to vocational training.

As far as a professional position goes, this is the lowest I've been. I was willing to accept this because I feel in the very near future, I will be back on top the way I was before. That's the way I feel. My ambition is to go on further and really be the head honcho in some situation.

My blindness may in some instances be a retardant. I might have been able to be involved in a situation where I wasn't given an opportunity because they felt I might have too many problems to deal with in order to be effective. Unless you know me and know my background, you might think it would be too much for me. But I believe that social programs or special interest programs will be even greater in the future. Being blind, whether I want to admit it or not, accept it or not, puts me in a special interest group. With my varied background and my blindness, it would tend to place me in a situation of authority. Basically, I'm counting on my blindness promoting me.

Not only as a blind person, but as a black person, I've been involved in a number of situations where I've been the only [one] or among the very few. My life has been a succession of proving myself. I'm competitive. I refuse to give up. I like the adulation that occurs afterwards. I honestly believe if it ever came to pass that blind [people] and blacks would be accepted by society, there would be other reasons why you have to prove yourself. I don't think society would ever be so accepting that one would not have to prove oneself. I don't think that is really a bad thing.

Jerry's message. I believe there'll always be differences. There'll always be those that will be different from the larger group. There will always be individuals having to prove themselves, having to gain respect from the larger group. I really don't have any message because I believe that this is the way it's gonna always be.

PARTIALLY SIGHTED (ALBINO)

JAN
(Institutional Administrator)

I met Jan at the Presbyterian Workshop on the Disabled. She is in her forties with striking white hair and light complexion. Her albinism is discussed on pages 119-122. Jan deals with the complications of being partially sighted. She can read print when it is held close to her eyes, but is technically defined as legally blind.

When I came in, you were sitting in the waiting room. I wasn't sure if it was you or not. That's the kind of problem a partially sighted person has. If I were totally blind you would understand that I wouldn't see you. People around here think I just ignore them.

I have 20/200 vision. That means that what you would see at 200 feet, I would have to be 20 feet away to see the same thing. Because of my albinism I'm also very sensitive to light. I have nystagmus which is the constant movement of my eyes. I also have strybismisus which means I just look out of one eye at a time. Because of that I don't have any depth perception. I didn't realize I didn't have depth perception all the time I was growing up. I had finished graduate school and I was on my first job when someone explained it to me. *I'm sure doctors I went to in childhood knew about it, but they just never thought to explain it to me.*

When I went to school, I had the feeling that I didn't see well; but it took me a while to understand I didn't see like other kids did. I remember being in the first grade about Christmas-time making Christmas cards for our parents. The teacher had written something on the blackboard. It was a long message, like, "Merry Christmas, Mother and Father."

We were supposed to copy that and take it up and show the teacher. When we got it good enough, she let us paste it into the little cards we had made. I don't remember how many times I went up there and never had it right. She got frustrated at one point and just shook me. She said, "I don't think you're ever going to learn how to write." I went home and told my mother about that. Out of that came the understanding that I couldn't see the blackboard from sitting way across the room. The teacher had to let me sit over by the blackboard.

I had glasses. Albinos don't normally get that much correction from glasses. I think glasses help the astigmatism a little bit. When I was a kid, I said I could read as well without the glasses as I could with them. The doctors had told my mother that she should always make sure I wore my glasses and she told me I had to. I'd wear them and break them playing ball. My parents were very poor. I'm sure it was an awful burden to have to keep fixing those glasses.

One of the problems I've always had was in sports activities. At recess when everybody was choosing up teams for playing ball, nobody wanted me on their team. That went a long way to feed into a monstrous inferiority complex I was building up. I wanted to play ball so bad. There was a scene in sixth grade. I went tearing into the teacher, saying, "Why don't you make them let me be on their team?" The teacher gave the whole class a lecture in front of me—the whole point of playing ball was not to win, but to have a good time. I was embarrassed. I was hurt. I wanted him to say something, but I guess I would have felt better if I had not been around when he said it. Looking back on it, he was right. He shouldn't talk behind my back. It probably didn't help 'cause, let's face it, when kids play ball they want to win, right? I understand that to a certain extent.

I had some friends. I was never really terribly popular. My

friends didn't understand my visual problem at all. Many times they didn't even want to acknowledge it. It was very puzzling to me when I was growing up, but I kind of understand it now. *I think it's a resistance to difference.* It's a feeling that, "I've been treating you like everybody else and you're telling me now you have a problem. That means I've got to take these things into consideration." It's just easier if you don't have a handicap—don't have a problem. They wanted to deny it.

I wanted to be an artist

I wanted to be an artist. When I went into high school, I was signed up for art five days a week. The second day I was in art class, a student came in and gave a note to the art teacher. The teacher said, "You're going to go to Latin class." "What! I'm supposed to go to Latin class?" He repeated, "You're not going to be in art class anymore." So I went to Latin class. My mother had gone to school and talked to the counselor and the dean of girls. They decided that if you don't see well, you shouldn't major in art. Nobody thought they should discuss that with me or give me my choices. I might have agreed with them, I don't know, but at least they should have talked to me. They shouldn't have sent a note with a student. I don't think they do things like that these days. I hope not.

It was a struggle

It was a struggle while I was growing up. I really didn't believe I was as smart as anybody else. I suppose that goes back to the first-grade teacher who said I'd never learn how to write. We were also very poor. That always fed into the feeling of being different and inferior.

I think adolescence was the worse time of my life—for all the reasons that adolescents have a hard time and because of the special problems of being visually handicapped. I had an inferiority complex. I really didn't have very many dates. I was a very passive person. It took me until my senior year in high school to learn that one of the reasons I wasn't popular was because I waited for things to come to me. That wasn't the way to get any place in life. You had to speak up and volunteer. I learned that too late in high school.

When I went to college, I lived at home so I missed out on a lot of social activities. At least I understood the reason then, in a different way than I did-when I was an adolescent. I understood that it was because I lived at home and we didn't have enough money for me to be in sororities and the social life.

To keep my State Rehab funding, I had to keep my grades up. I read so slowly. I spent almost all my time in books. I had some reader service, but I wasn't used to it. This is one of the problems people with low vision have. You get used to large print or using magnifying glasses. In college you have an enormous amount of reading that you just can't cope with. But to suddenly switch to a reader you have to get it through the ears instead of the eyes. You have to go at the reader's pace.

These days it's easier with the small tape recorders. You give your book to the reader and he reads it at his convenience. If you don't understand it, you don't feel embarrassed about having to go back over that sentence three or four times.

I've done a lot of what I want to do. I went to college, despite the fact that lots of people said I couldn't make it. I went to graduate school. I even graduated from college *magna cum laude*.

She had to prove herself in the sighted community

I had a fellowship in graduate school which committed me to work for two years in a rehab agency for the blind. I was interested in doing that but I wasn't sure I could get a job anyplace but an agency for the blind. As soon as my two years were up, I was out looking for another job. I got a job working in a hospital. That was a kind of proof to me that I could get a job in a place other than an agency for the blind. I thought I was proving it to the world, but now I know I was proving it to myself.

That job didn't work out because the director of social services was unprofessional. I left the hospital and worked in a rehab hospital. I was back into the feeling that, sure, a place for the handicapped would hire the handicapped. I made up my mind that I was going to look for another job.

I got a job as a special project worker at Episcopal Community Services. Then I was promoted from straight case worker to supervisor. I really got my proof that I could work in an agency that didn't have anything to do with the handicapped.

I am now associate director of Nevil Institute of Rehabilitation Services. I'd been on my job at ECS for twelve years. Because of administrative changes, that job had become unpleasant. I kept feeling the pull that I ought to get back into services for the blind. I kept saying, "No," but I knew I wanted to get out of my old job. So I took this job saying I'd take it for a year; if I didn't like it, I'd get out.

I've been so happy with this job because I've gotten a lot of things worked out inside myself. Also the field has changed a little bit. When I was working in an agency for the blind early in my career, I felt a constant pull to be one or the other. You know how society has to put everybody into a category to understand. Since I have 20/200 vision, I am legally blind. In recent years there's a lot more recognition of partially sighted, or as they call it now, low vision. The people with low vision really are all the things that I always thought I was. That in-between category that nobody could really understand because our needs are different from the sighted and different from the blind. I didn't want to be labeled blind because of the stereotypes I had that everybody else does about blindness, and also I knew that it wasn't me.

I think lots of people assume I can't see anything. With all the consciousness raising these days, when I make it known that I don't see well, they'll keep insisting that I should be brailled. I can't read braille so I'm much worse off than I am with print. At least with a magnifying glass, I can get something out of print.

There's a supervisor who works under me who really has a tremendous ability to remember little things that I don't expect people to remember. For example, when we go into a restaurant, if we're going to sit down at a table and one of us has to face a window with a lot of bright light, she just automatically remembers. "You need to sit over there." I don't expect people to remember those kinds of things. I don't even expect my husband to remember little things like that. He does sometimes and he doesn't. Reesa has an unusual ability. I really appreciate it. It's a good feeling.

Are people generally helpful?

No, not very. When I was in New York and riding the subways a lot, I'd ask people, "Is this the E train?" "Yes." You'd get on it and find much later it's not the E train at all. A mobility trainer told somebody that's never the way you ask questions. You say, *"What train is this?"* It forces the person you're asking to look and give you an answer. If you ask them a yes or no question, they'll almost always answer, "Yes."

Bus terminals are just terrible. If I can't see what bus it is and there's nobody around to ask, I have to get on the bus and say, "Is this such and such a bus?" The bus drivers will say, "What's a matter, lady, can't you see?" I'll say very sweetly, "As a matter of fact, I don't see very well. That's why I'm asking you." "Well, lady, why don't you get a new pair of glasses?" This is not a joke to them. They're very serious and very angry about it. One time I got on the bus with a woman driver. Cute little black lady. I thought, *This is neat. I bet you anything women bus drivers will be more compassionate to the public.* Suddenly I realized everybody was getting off, and the bus ride had ended before I expected. I went to the driver and asked if she could give me a free transfer for the next bus. She said, "What's the matter, can't you see? The stop is on the bus in plain sight." I thought, *There goes my theory that women are going to be more compassionate with the handicapped than men are.*

The telescopic lens

These days there is a whole optical field called "low-vision." They come up with lots of low-vision aids. This is a bioptic.* When I was at the workshop on the disabled in the church and they were writing on the blackboard, I kept thinking, "Why don't I get out my bioptic and wear it?" I never did. Later in the afternoon when they showed a movie, I put it on. I have lots of trouble wearing this because I have so many hang-ups that I don't want to look crazy. I think this is really weird looking. If you wear it on the street, you get all kinds of weird response. I have a very good friend who is supervisor of case workers and rehab teachers. He wears one of these. He had some feelings like mine when he first got it, but his vision is a lot worse than mine and he gets marvelous correction with it. I carry mine around and I put it on when it's going to really help me. He wears his all the time and he's had all kinds of crazy experiences. People assume it's a jewelers' glass for one thing and they come up to him and start talking about diamonds. One women came up and shoved her engagement ring in his face and said, "Can you tell me whether this is worth anything?"

My first experience in wearing it in public and getting a really awful response was in the airport. Reesa [a co-worker] went into the terminal with me and walked up to the desk with me. I was wearing the bioptic because I have trouble in airports in seeing the TV screen with the schedules. We walked up to the check-in point. The girl who was processing my luggage couldn't understand the bioptic. She did something that had never happened to me before, but it happens to blind people all the time. First, she assumed that because I was wearing this weird thing, I was blind. And because I was blind, I couldn't talk. She kept talking to Reesa. The girl kept saying, "Are you going to stay with her? Should I assign a ground escort for her?" I didn't understand what was going on. Reesa under-

---

*Telescopic lens

stood before I did. She finally just said, "Look, this is an intelligent woman. She is my supervisor and she knows what she is doing and she can see. Would you stop talking to me and start talking to her!"

One of the things that annoys me most about this whole business of the handicapped is that we have to work so hard on our feelings about wearing strange devices that are going to help us. This thing really helps me. If I had the guts to put it on that day of the disabled workshop, I probably could have seen that blackboard and then I wouldn't have had to put anyone through reading that stuff to me. I don't blame the public entirely. It's partly my own vanity that I won't wear it.

Jan's message. Don't make judgments about people just because they're different. Don't get scared because of the difference. I worked for years in an agency for the blind. When I meet a blind person, I still don't automatically know the right thing for them. Don't feel like you should be expected to know what to do for a handicapped person. When they get angry at you because you've done the wrong thing, that may be some of their own hang-ups about their handicap. Just keep in mind when dealing with handicapped people, it's all right to ask how you can help.

TIM
(A Graduate Student)

Tim is a graduate student in psychology.

I'm albino. I have a really light complexion, white hair, white eyebrows, pale features, and a sort of pink tone to my skin. If I'm in a situation where I have to read something, then I'll bring it up to my nose almost. I'll walk right up to a street sign and peer up at it. That's when I'm very noticeable.

It's genetic, inherited. I have an aunt on my father's side who has a lesser degree of albinism than I do. I think my brother's child has predominantly occular albinism. He has some vision problems, but that's the extent of it.

I was first aware of it in first or second grade. My parents were concerned about my being in a school where they could take care of my needs. I had to sit close to the front and walk up and stand by the blackboard. I went to a private school. They didn't have any special education classes or cater to people with vision problems, but the classes were smaller.

I couldn't do things the other students did. I had particular difficulty with sports because I wanted to do a lot of sports. That was a big thing in the school. I did play baseball but I couldn't really be involved in a lot of the action because I couldn't see the ball. The kids were okay, but there were a lot of jokes. I was aware of having white hair and a light complexion especially because I'm so sensitive to the sun. There were jokes about Santa Claus or snowmen. But for the most part it was done innocently. It wasn't meant to be hurtful. It did hurt—not each time, but just the whole idea that I was in a situation where I would have jokes made about me. In grade school, I just figured the jokes were a way I got attention. This is how I feel accepted and I'm going to go with it. But by the same token, you have to stand up at some point and say, "That's enough." I'm a different person. I'm not just an albino and I don't just have white hair.

They really wanted to know

It would have been helpful if it had been discussed in class. At one point, some kid in class—out of the blue almost—raised his hand and said, "Sister, what is albinism? What is albino?" She spoke for maybe ten minutes. I felt really good about that. The class seemed to listen. I got the sense that they really wanted to know and they could accept it and understand. There was a different feeling after that. It took me out of the aura of being different—took the edge of mystery off it. That made me more of a regular person.

Adolescence was hard

I would say adolescence was hard. There were ways in which I felt inadequate. I felt incapable of doing things. Because of that it generalized and I felt inadequate. I didn't feel like a leader-type person, the kid who was the center of the group, talking a lot, having a lot of friends, lots of things to do. I didn't feel comfortable suggesting ideas and expecting that people would say, "Hey, that's a good idea. I'll come along." I felt I had to wait for people to come up to me and say, "Why don't you come and do this?" I was scared of not succeeding.

I'm a psychology major, and I've been constantly thinking about my past and how I was raised and what my parents did. I think they could have done more to make things easier for me. To try and help me cope. They didn't really talk to me in depth, in a feeling way. That would have been helpful—to explore things with me. I got most of my education about albinism by going to eye doctors and through reading a little bit. I probably knew more about it genetically and organically by eighth grade than my parents did. They knew it is genetic, it's inherited, but I don't know if they would say it's recessive. My mother always said, "We asked the doctor and he said if you just marry a girl with dark skin, you won't have to worry about having albino children." In a sense it holds, but it doesn't really. So there was that kind of superficial knowledge on their part. They tried to give me what they knew, but I think they were encouraged by doctors and other people to let me find my own way.

I have difficulty with dependence

I am willing to compromise my needs when I'm with people in order not to make the situation uncomfortable. If I were in a fast food place with the menu right above me, someone might be reading the menu to themselves and selecting something. Since I couldn't read the menu, I might just select the popular item just not to feel uncomfortable saying, "Hey, can you read the menu to me?" I would just go along with something I knew or something I might have heard about on TV. For me, it's the most comfortable, but in some situations I lose out. I have difficulty with dependence on people. I would rather feel really independent.

I do like it when there's someone I know really well and I'll say, "Hey, what's that say?" or "What's going on over there?" Because I do like to know. But when I'm with someone I don't know as well, I won't, because I would rather they think that I'm just as capable as they are. A goal for me while I'm interacting with people is to be able to act as if I don't have any special needs or to be able to show that I've got them under control. If I feel comfortable bringing a newspaper really close to my face to be able to read, then I can externalize it. There it is. This is how I deal with it and that's fine. Then I can still do everything else the way you do it. That's the goal for me. That keeps the separateness about it.

I'm wanting to expand the realm of things I do. I just went golfing for the first time the other day. I had a great time. The person I was with knew I would have difficulty following the ball. He was really helpful initially—the first four or five holes. He would watch for my shots and guide me to where the ball was. Then he started to get into the game himself and was going off on his own a little bit. I was becoming frustrated. It started to become a drag. I wound up losing a lot of my balls. I told a girlfriend afterwards that I'd love to do it again, but would she spot balls for me and she said, "Sure." I would feel comfortable with her. I get a sense sometimes that I'm intruding on other people when I lay all my needs on them like that.

The telescopic lens

I have reading glasses but I only use them for close-up reading and if I'm going to be sitting for a long time. I just recently got a telescopic type devise which is on a regular reading glass frame. This telescope is about an inch long and one inch in diameter. I wear it occasionally. I've only had it a week. I'm not quite comfortable wearing it all the time. I can use it really well and I can see better with it. When I first had it on, I wasn't as uncomfortable as I expected to be. A curious reason is because I finally was able to see what people were looking at more clearly. I found out they really weren't looking at me and I felt better about that. If I were more on show, I don't think I would have felt as comfortable.

For so long I've gotten by on not really seeing what people do at distances. Now I almost feel like I have an insider's view or special powers. It is so rewarding and so remarkable now that I can see so much. It makes the cosmetic thing about wearing a telescope seem trivial.

I appreciate that people will look at me because I look at other people who for one reason or another stand out. Just to satisfy the curiosity. They've never seen an albino before. If they take a second look, that's fine, but not to stare. Not to turn around again and play the staring game where they'll stare and I'll catch them and they'll look down and then do it again. Don't do that.

A lot of people ask me, "What color are your eyes?" and they'll wanta take a look. There are albinos who might have pink eyes. It's not that they really have pink eyes, but due to the severity of their condition, they have so little pigment in their body that the light goes into their eyes and reflects back out. The pink color you see is a reflection of the blood flowing through the eye. That can happen.

It's only a drawback as far as I let it be

I would like to do consultations, therapy, supervising, maybe crisis intervention, basically all revolving around psychology. I can see ways in which my albinism will be a help. I'm more insightful generally and probably more sensitive to people dealing with major things in their lives because of having to do that throughout my whole life. I think that's left me with a real talent for counseling. There's that trade-off. It's only a drawback as far as I let it be. If I don't get over all the hang-ups, and I don't completely come to terms with it, and accept it, then it'll be a drawback.

It would be okay if my children were albino. I would have a different kind of connection with that child. I would take more of a special interest in helping that child learn to cope in a better way. I would share some of the funny situations that I incur because of it and I know they would understand more clearly than someone else would. If I knew the woman I was going to marry carried the recessive gene for albinism, that would not be a reason not to marry her. It wouldn't affect my having children.

Tim's message to other albinos. Just be aware of what you can do and let other people know what you can do. Don't be afraid to ask people to fill in the gaps for you. Be able to separate. I'm partially sighted, but that's something separate—that's not *me*.

PARTIALLY SIGHTED

GENE
(A Clerk-Typist)

Gene has been partially sighted since birth. Recently he has begun to wear a telescopic lens attached to his glasses. The lens, which is approximately one inch thick, enables Gene to see objects which he has never seen before. When asked if he feels self-conscious wearing an object which attracts attention, he shrugs his shoulders and says good-naturedly, "Maybe I'm a show-off. You never know. I just feel what you've got to do, you've got to do."

I was a rubella baby.* My mother had a rash and had extreme emotional problems because my father was an alcoholic. When I was born, I had cataracts. Plus, my eyes are not the normal size. They also had to put me in oxygen because I was premature.

I resented being in a school for the blind

I started in at the school for the blind. I didn't like the school a whole lot. As far as I was concerned, the only things I liked were the music programs and the teachers. To me it was a very barren type of situation. There was no feeling of acceptance. I think, partly, too, I could see, and I resented being in a school for the blind when I could see.

Then I went to public school and was in sight-conservation

---

*German measles, which if contracted in the first trimester of pregnancy may lead to birth defects.

classes. I went to about ninth grade and then I had to drop out because they didn't have anything in high school in Washington to support a partially sighted person. So I went to work. I picked up things on the side and finally I took a G.E.D. test, passed it, and kept on working until 1954 when I started college. I went to junior college first to try my luck, and then to Wilson College in North Carolina. I went from there to Berea College in Kentucky, finished there, and went to the University of Kentucky to get my master's degree in history.

Would you recommend that a partially sighted person go to a school for the blind or to a special sight-saving class in public school?

I would say it depended on the family situation. If the family situation is a wholesome one where the person feels he is part of the family, knows he is wanted and accepted—and it is important to him that he stay with the family and it's important to the family that he stay with them—I would probably say the sight-saving conservation situation would be good.

What to do with myself . . .

My teenage years were not particularly difficult for me. I didn't do some of the things teenagers did. I made up for that by my interest in history. I got my head stuck in that. My problem was one of trying to figure out what to do with myself after I got to be 18. I had a lot of counseling. I was lucky in that respect. I went to Family and Child Service Agency in Washington and I ran into a real sharp gal there. She worked with me along the way. They used Carl Rogers' method mainly—bounced the idea off. That helped a lot, because it made my mind slowly begin to activate. That's when I got my high school diploma. That was a very good example.

I try to maintain an "up" attitude

I'm a clerk-typist with the Delaware County Board of Assistance. I take preliminary interviews over the phone for people who are homebound and then I send a form on to another worker who goes to see them. The office atmosphere is very bad because so many people are down and are sarcastic in their approach to life. I try to maintain a sort of up attitude with myself if I can. Because if I don't, when I have trouble, it knocks me pretty hard. I've got to build on whatever I've got.

The sight problem is a factor at work. They are very myopic in their attitude toward physically handicapped people. They don't realize that blind people are capable of doing the things that the Federal Government has been able to do with them— such as doing social security interview work. They don't give me enough responsibility for the level of education that I have, and for what I feel I could do. I'm trying to get a little more proficient job.

Do you get a reaction from people when you wear your telescopic lens?

People are in such a hurry that they don't give a reaction. Kids will. Kids tease me about it. "What's the telescope? What are you looking for?" It doesn't bother me. I tell them what it is. I tell an older person it's a "lecher's lens."

I want to see better and I don't care how I look. To me that's important. I wear it everywhere. That's my baby. I don't care if people look at me. That's their privilege. It doesn't worry me. That's how much I like to see. I want to enjoy it while I can.

We listen to books

I can't play baseball and I don't play football. We* mainly listen to books. I guess our favorite activity is listening to books. We listen to anything—murder mysteries mainly, espionage, and a good love story. We get our books from the Library of the Blind and Physically Handicapped downtown.

We're active in our church. There is just one other girl who is blind. They treat us pretty well. We have a good relationship

---

*Gene's wife is blind

with the minister and his wife. I am a Reinhold Niebuhr theologian.

I used to think that God had something in store for me, particularly when I started getting on—getting my high school diploma, going to college. I think he probably has a path for me, but I don't know what it is—now. Maybe I was trying to read God's mind which is a bad thing to try to do. Right now I take the attitude that I'm very glad I got my education, very glad I've got what I got, and maybe I'm not using it as well as I should. Something may happen that may come my way. In fact, Chuck (the minister) said he would keep an eye open for any teaching jobs in Christian schools.

I thought for a while when I got married, "Did I do the right thing? Should I have remained single and maybe sacrificed and tried it alone?" But I'm very happy being married. My wife puts up with me. She's helped me, given me a lot of encouragement. She knew what my problems were. I think that was the big factor. Because she is blind, she knew what my problems were. She didn't think I was a goof-off because I didn't have work for a long time. She knew it was very difficult for a blind person to find employment.

Gene's message. I would like society to allow people to apply for jobs and get employment as *persons*—not as blind persons or partially sighted persons or as hearing-aid wearing persons or anything like that. I'm a human being and everybody has something. A person ought to be treated as an individual and not be given exclusionary treatment or overly inclusive treatment. He should be given an opportunity to be a human being.

JACK (A Volunteer)

Jack is partially sighted as a result of having a variant of Hurler's syndrome. He explains that the true Hurlers is a total breakdown of tissues in the whole body. The only other feature he has, besides his eye problem, is his hands. They are small for his stature. As his eyesight became progressively worse through high school and his early twenties, he experienced fear and anxiety. Jack describes how he got through that period.

During grade school and the beginning of high school I was able to read regular print. I went to regular schools. I always sat up front by the blackboard. I had free-roaming rights of the schoolroom. I could just get up and change my seat. The teachers didn't understand it, but they didn't question it. The teachers were my biggest problem. They didn't know how to treat me. They didn't know how much I could see. The biggest problem is ignorance. People just simply don't understand what it's all about.

I started to go downhill in high school, about my sophomore year. I had more trouble reading print.

I remember one incident. I had gym class my sophomore year and our gym teacher was an ex-drill sergeant in the marine corps. He was pretty tough. He would have us line up. The bleachers were pushed up against the wall and they were numbered. I had to stand in front of number four. I simply couldn't see number four. He grabbed me by my hair and dragged me up to where the number four was and then he pointed to it. He ran my hand down the side of the bleacher, across the floor, and up to where I'm supposed to be standing. I never got over that. To this day, I still hold a grudge.

I had a really bad day

[After high school] I was working for a printing company. I was having trouble, but not that bad. I could fight my way through it. One day in October 1972, I had a really bad day. Before that, the day would start out and my eyes would be really blurry for a few hours and as the day went on, they would clear up. One day I got up and went to work and I never cleared up, and it's been that way since. It came on me just like that. I had to proofread as part of my job. Needless to say, I quit the job.

I was scared. I was terrorized. I didn't know what was happening. I went through a period of drinking—hard drinking. It was a combination of not knowing what to expect, plus I felt lonely. I knew that people were concerned about me, but I *felt* like they didn't care.

I went to work for a trucking company. I worked from 6:00 at night to 3:00 in the morning. I used to get up about 3:30 in the afternoon, wouldn't eat a thing, just go straight to the corner bar, sit there and drink until it was time to go to work. I went to work several times, not plastered, but tipsy. I had a boss who kinda understood what I was going through and he didn't say anything. He just gave me a cup of coffee, sat me down, and said, "When you're ready to go to work, just go to your desk."

A friend of mine recognized that I had a problem and he approached me. He said he was having a few problems himself and he'd been going up to a retreat in New York—a private Catholic retreat. So I tagged along with him just for anyhow. I went up there for weekend trips for about a year. It brought me to a realization that what will be will be. That helped. Everybody had been afraid to come forward and say, "Jack, you need help." This one chap finally did have the courage.

I met Susan

I worked for the trucking company for two years until I couldn't do anything there anymore and then I went to the state for help. They sent me to the Upsal Center for the Blind. I went through mobility training. I learned braille which I have since forgotten. I didn't know how bad my eyesight was going to get. Then they sent me to Little Rock to the Arkansas Enterprises for the Blind. They had several agencies within the government where they would train blind or partially sighted individuals for information type of work such as IRS. A lot of their taxpayer service representatives are blind and partially sighted. I was training for the civil service commission. And that's where I met Susan. She was from Tennessee and she was down there for the same training.

She went to Kansas City for her job and I came back to Philadelphia. Then she transferred here when we got married. I didn't think about her being blind. Didn't think about it. That wasn't taken into consideration at all. Our first date was on July 1 and I asked her to marry me on September 8, just over two months later. I guess I knew we would run up against a lot of things, but we really haven't. Susan has an advantage in that she saw at one time. She was hurt in an accident when she was 18.

Susan's not too crazy about parties. She never did like crowds. The biggest problem she has—she doesn't like attention brought to her. Ninety-nine percent of our friends just take Susan for Susan. That's just Susan. That's not blind Susan—that's just Susan.

We have run into situations where we've been to a social occasion and somebody will come up and say, "Do you know who this is?" And everybody will turn around and look and Susan knows everybody's looking. If she guesses wrong, everybody will say, "Ahhhh." Her biggest hang-up about being at a party is people drawing attention to her because of her blindness. She doesn't like that. And I'm not too thrilled about it myself.

One of my uncles passed away recently. We went to the viewing. Susan and I were sitting there and she was on the outside of the little row of seats. We had a lot of cousins and relatives come up. I noticed that most of them came up to Susan and said, "Hi, Susan. It's Jane. How are you?" or "Hi, Susan, it's Joe." I thought that was terrific. It's good to identify yourself.

Should I or shouldn't I?

People help me too much all the time. A lot of times, depending on who the person is, I'll either let them just go ahead and do it, or if it's a good friend, I'll just tell them, "Get outta here." That kind of thing. If I really needed help, I'd rather get too much. I run into that a lot when I go shopping. One time I hadda look for some flavor of Jell-O my wife wanted to bake a cake. Of course a Jell-O packet has the name in red and I have a really hard time seeing red printing. I'll tell by the design of the fruit on the box or the color of the fruit. Older ladies are the greatest because they'll stand there and they'll watch and you can tell they're debating, "Should I, or shouldn't I?" So what I'll do a lot of times if I really do need the help, I'll say, "Excuse me, will you tell me which one of these is blueberry?" or whatever. I get, "Honey, I didn't know whether to ask you or not. I knew you were having problems." I'll just go right along with them. I walk away feeling good because I know they feel good.

At one time I would have rejected it. I've heard several stories and I've run into it myself with the totally blind, especially. A person is waiting to cross the street and you go up to him and say, "Can I help you cross the street?" "Nah!" That kind of gives Joe Smith off the street a bad impression. He may walk down the street the next day and see a girl having a bit of a problem and he won't approach her. She's hoping that somebody will approach her. So it's got to work both ways. The next guy may need it.

Jack's message. What I'd like to tell people is no matter who you are, whether it shows or not, there is something wrong with you. Whether it's physical or mental. It may never come out. But I guarantee there's something wrong with you—whether it be your eyes, your hearing, a back problem. There's something wrong with everybody. And you've got to take into consideration that what somebody else has, is always worse than what you have.

If I start to get a little bit depressed, I'll turn around and I'll look at other people. I'll see somebody walking down the street—not walking, but riding down the street in a wheelchair—and I think, that could be me. I'm happy with what I have. I'm happy that this is all I have.

Words, words, words.
   —Hamlet

   So much comes through your speech. That's probably more than any part of you. It would almost be the same if you were forced to walk around in rags or half naked. You would feel self-conscious all the time. Stuttering has the same effect. You're always putting your worst foot forward.
   —George

   To speak or not to speak, that is the stutterer's vital question.
   —Charles VanRiper, in Speech Correction

   I am slow of speech, and of a slow tongue.
   —Moses (Exodus 4:10)

SPEECH

Stuttering, Aphasia

Over 6 percent of the United States population has a speech handicap. Those who do not receive correction go through life "at a serious disadvantage vocationally, socially, and in intimate personal ways" (Perkins, *Speech Pathology*, p. 3).

Stuttering is one of the more complex disorders of speech. Its cause and correction are continually being debated. Regardless of its cause, it is a socially handicapping problem. In childhood the stutterer endures the taunting and teasing by those who, suffering insecurity in themselves, have found vulnerable victims. That problem gradually abates to some extent in maturity. But then people eager to put one at ease, may try to supply the blocked word or phrase. "Occasionally this happens and though I appreciate their feelings toward me, they might say the wrong thing. Then you not only gotta correct what they say, but then you gotta say it right" (George). Judith advises, "I'd like people not to get anxious about it."

There are different types of aphasia and a study is necessary to define the terms. It will simply be stated here that adult aphasia is usually caused by a stroke and results in a disruption of language processes. It is frightening for a recovering stroke victim to search for a word and not be able to find it. For three weeks after her stroke, Janet did not know if she would ever be able to talk or not. She says, "That's why now I go to the hospital and tell other aphasia patients that they can get better."

There are many other speech problems, some are correctable by therapy or surgery. In the meantime, we should relax and listen to what the person has to say, not how he says it.

Aphasia: Aphasia is a result of brain damage, usually from a stroke. The aphasic has difficulty formulating, comprehending, or expressing meanings. Often there is some impairment in all of these three functions. Along with these difficulties there may be associated problems of defective articulation, inability to produce voice, and broken fluency; but the basic problem lies in handling symbolic behavior.

Stuttering: Stuttering is when the forward flow of speech is interrupted by mistiming to such an extent that it becomes conspicuous and interferes with communication. There is no single cause for stuttering, but there are three different theories of its origin: the learning theory, the neurotic theory, and the theory of constitutional difference. Stuttering can often be helped by speech therapy.

STUTTERING

JUDITH (A Biologist)

Judith is an attractive woman who has been in speech therapy most of her life for stuttering. She reminds us that stuttering is a problem, but it is not the person. "I'm still me!"

My major difference is that I stutter. My speech is—*was*—really horrendous, especially as a child. It's a lot better now after years and years of therapy. But there was a point in time, especially when I was small, that I couldn't say two words without having a bad block. It's a strange kind of handicap. It's a socially punishable handicap.

I started stuttering when I was two and a half. It had a rather abrupt onset. I'm told—I don't remember this—in about a week I went from being as *fluent* as any child that age ever is, to being all tied up in knots. My mother felt *terrible* about it because she had left me to go to my dad who was in an army hospital. It was during the six-week period that she was gone that I started to stutter and she felt it was her fault. You know how mothers are. When I came to meet her at the plane and I couldn't talk, she said her heart dropped right down to the bottom of her shoes.

I don't recall a time when I didn't have trouble talking. I must have been aware of it even at two and one half years because I had terrible times. I practically turned myself inside out trying to talk. Besides, my grandmother, particularly, was always on my case about, "Now, stop, take a deep breath."

My mother was always aware that I had a problem, but she never made me feel I was not acceptable on account of it. I was not acceptable for other problems, but not on account of speech that I couldn't help. She wasn't always hounding me about it, anyway. She encouraged me, of course, and she took me to speech therapy, but she didn't try to do any herself—for which I was *profoundly* grateful. She never gave me techniques to handle. And she never appeared impatient when I had trouble with words. *Adults who don't know anything about speech therapy—which is the majority—have no idea how to tackle it and they give you all kinds of "help" that is no help. Better it should be left to someone who knows what they're doing.*

School was terrible—terrible

School was terrible. Talking in class was horrendous. I had trouble with that from kindergarten on, but it became really bad by the third or fourth grade when you had to talk in class to get a good grade. You had to answer questions. I would never raise my hand—never.

I got good grades because of my written work. Some of the teachers called on me. Some of them, after they heard me talk, didn't. I appreciated it when they didn't ask me. I used to have bad dreams about trying to talk in front of a class—especially if I had to stand in front of a class. I would almost die of embarrassment.

I never volunteered, but when I was called on, I would try to answer the question. But in junior high school, I started going up to every new teacher at the start of the semester and explain that I had a speech defect and would they please not call on me in class. It got harder and harder to talk in class. As I got older, I got more and more self-conscious about it and it began to be so bad that I would go into class when I was afraid of being called on in such a state of anxiety that I was all tensed up. My palms would sweat, I would really be in terrible shape. I felt so bad about asking to get out of something that everybody else did and that I ought to do, too. But I could not face going to class every day with that anxiety. I just couldn't stand it. I just had to try to ease the anxiety a little bit. So I used to go up—as hard as it was and as guilty as I felt—and ask the teachers if they could please excuse me. The majority of them did. I just couldn't stand to have my defect on display like that. I just didn't have the courage.

Look, I was a good student

I think the teacher's reaction depends on the child. The whole child. I'm not just a speech problem. There was a whole personality that was quite shy, quite timid, very, very afraid— very high anxiety level, for everything. I think for the kind of child I was, when I got to the point as I did in early junior high where it was so painful, I think school would have been unendurable if I had had to face day in and day out the possibility of being called on in any and all classes.

Occasionally a teacher would ask me a question that could be answered by one word, and that was nice. But the teacher has to make a judgment on the basis of the individual child.

I think with me, it would not have helped to be made to talk, because I don't think I could have stood it. School was hard enough as it was. But as long as I could do so well in written work—and I did—I got As mostly, then, all right, I could still keep that. Look, I was a good student. Being a good student has meant a tremendous amount in my life. I went to graduate school. I got a master's degree. I went into lab work. Supposing they had made me talk and I had been unable to reach my potential because of the much greater anxiety or because I would say, "I won't go to school. I just can't stand it any longer. I'll kill myself." And I had that in mind from an extremely young age. And I might have done just that, I mean, there was a risk. A risk of pushing me beyond endurance and I might have taken my life. Besides, I think it would have robbed me of being the kind of student I was.

Toward the end of high school, I began, on my own, to talk in class again—occasionally. I still had a terrible time, but I started to do it. When I went to college, even more so, especially in classes that interested me.

Kids made fun of me innumerable times. I probably got less than a lot of kids because I was sensitive and it showed. High school adolescent boys are just about the cruelest people in the human species—at least, in my experience. But if the teacher caught them, they got slapped down real quick, which I appreciated no end. But kids were usually smart enough not to let adults hear.

Kids and adolescents do not trust and are not comfortable with those who are not like them, those they know they can hurt. To some children, that is like a red flag. If they know they can hurt you, they're gonna try to do it.

Strangers . . . oh, boy. Today I still have the same problem. A stranger—I'm scared to death they're not going to accept me, they're not going to like me. They're gonna think I'm weird. They're gonna think I'm retarded. Even one of my high school teachers thought I was retarded [laughs]. I have a much higher than normal I.Q., but he didn't know the difference between speech and mental retardation. But people don't know, they really don't. They hear somebody who can't talk and they assume that she can't think any more than she can talk. They may speak more slowly and succinctly [laughs] as if I were hard of hearing, because they don't know.

I was more fluent with my close friends and when I wasn't fluent I didn't have to worry about it because they weren't going to throw me over. They liked me in spite of it. Some of them would comment on it occasionally, but most of them would accept me no matter how hard a time I had. They liked me for me in spite of my speech.

That's what a friend is for [laughs]: in spite of your problems, they like you anyway. There's enough in me to like that many people will ignore the speech, especially after they get to know me.

Judith chose her profession of biology because it was one in which she would not be judged by her speech.

I decided two years ago that I would go into psychology and try because I was more interested in it. But I decided it was more trouble than it was worth. I did *splendidly;* but speech-wise, it wasn't going to work. So now I'm back in biology. The Lord works in mysterious ways. If he wants me to be with people, he'll throw a job in my way that will enable me to do that. I work alone in a lab, and it does get boring. You do the same thing over and over again. You don't have the challenge of being with people. I would be tempted to change to psychology if my speech ever got really, really fluent so that I could count on it with all people, not just with somebody I could know a little, like you. I'm a *long* way from being able to make a phone call to a perfect stranger . Any job where you'd have to make calls, I'd be at a *terrible* disadvantage. I have a terrible time with phones. My speech would have to be practically indistinguishable from normal—which I kinda doubt that it will ever be.

Don't get anxious about it

There's a large variety of reactions from strangers. I don't want them to say the word when I'm hesitating. I have to say the word myself. Besides, half the time they're wrong anyway [laughs]. They assume they know what I'm going to say. I prefer to do my own talking. I was trained that way. In fact, it's the only way to do it because I know what I want to say.

I'd like people not to get anxious about it. That's what I'd like most. Because they do. It's normal because they don't know what to do. They're confronted with somebody—they may never have heard an adult stutterer before because we're not all that common. Most of us are underground. We don't talk to people. We don't mingle with people. I try to go to a store where I can get what I want off the counter. If I have to ask, then I ask. But this morning I had to ask for earplugs. As I was walking toward the drugstore, I got nervous. I was not near panic, but my anxiety level perceptably got quite high. But I knew I could do it. I knew the druggist slightly and I knew he would not interrupt. He would not try to say it. He heard me talk at least a couple times before.

A lot of black people—I don't usually see racial differences—respond much more the way I like than a lot of whites. Not as anxious about it. This is a generalization, of course, but the best reactions to my speech from people who are hearing it for the first time have been from black people. There's not an air of "What's the matter with her?" or the anxiety, "How can I help her talk?" They look at me like everybody does when they first hear me have a bad block, but it's sort of, "Now, I wonder what's happening here?" and a much quicker realization that I *stutter*. It's part of life that all people don't do all things well. I just happen to have a problem with speech and it's sort of a relaxed atmosphere and acceptance. It's going to take me longer and they'll wait and so what. It's not the end of the world. That's the kind of reaction I like.

People need to be set at ease

You were asking how I hoped others would react to me and what I think is extremely important is how *I* act with them. How somebody with the problem reacts to other people. During the years when my speech was much worse and I was having a terrible time, I felt really bad about it and I devalued myself in my own eyes. I felt uncomfortable and anxious. That *always* makes the other person feel more anxious than he was. I came to understand that I have as much to say as the next person but it just takes me longer to say it, but it's well worth hearing. If I want them to react to me primarily as a person who just happens to have a problem and not as just one big problem, then it's my job, too, to approach them as a person whose problem is just a minor thing. But, it's not *me*. Especially in recent years, I do present myself more as a person not so terribly handicapped. And that really works wonders. You can't control it, but at least you can contribute to the best possible response on the other person. And people do need to be set at ease.

All the people that you meet are not going to approve of you. No matter what you are. They may not like the color of your hair or your eyes or maybe you remind them of their dad and they hated their father [laughs]. Maybe something as strange as that, but some people are just going to not like you for something totally beyond your control. There's something analogous with this kind of a problem to say, racism. Some people will look at black people and automatically say that person is not a person. He's not really a person like I am. Sociologists call that "outgroup stereotyping."

Some people feel that way about Jews, of which I am one. They don't think we're people. Trying to expect everybody in the world to accept you with no problems is a pipe dream. It can't be done. Okay, it's not your fault. It just happens that not all people are ever going to respond in a favorable way to you. If you have a handicap, it's wise to be aware of that, not to look for it. Some people look for prejudice and when you look for it, you're apt to find it.

If I had a wish . . .

If I had a wish, the thing that's closest to my heart, above anything else, I want a closer walk with God. That's *the* major thing in my life. Speech, my bad back, my ulcer, anything is minor in comparison. That's so far ahead, it's in a class by itself. I'm in a messianic synagogue. I'm a Christian Jew. We're strong on healing and I pray for healing all the time. I think he *is* healing me. But my speech is a long, slow thing. I believe in healing, but I believe that God allows us to have problems for purposes of instruction in this life.

Judith's message. People are people first. People have problems. Some of them are obvious. Some of them are not so obvious. But if you come across a person with an obvious problem, look at the person, not the problem. The problem is not the whole of the individual. The person is what's important.

As far as specifics, yes, I like the fact that most people are anxious to help if they can, but don't be too anxious. Don't try to talk my words. I've gotta speak for myself. Don't look at me like I'm some kind of freak. I'm different, but I'm more like you than I'm not like you. I just happen to have this one area where I'm obviously not "normal," but that's a very small part of me as a person. Don't make it the major part of me.

GEORGE (A Psychologist)

George is a young man who works in a rehabilitation center as a psychologist. He stuttered severely as a young child, but his stuttering is barely perceptible now. He tells of his experiences and his treatment.

In some cases there could be an organic basis [for stuttering]. I don't know if that's the explanation in all cases. I have mixed dominance. I've always been a left-handed writer, yet I do a lot of things with my right hand. I still don't honestly know if forcing a person to use his right hand fits in with the mixed dominance idea. Nobody ever tried to force me. I always wrote with my left hand. My father always thought I was trained to be too timid. Even if a person isn't timid, stuttering tends to make him look like a timid, weak person. Knowing the cause doesn't provide any practical tools by which you can do anything about it. The biggest help is to actually learn something that will help you get through the tight situations.

I had a problem stuttering in kindergarten. I was aware of it since "Show and Tell" where you have to bring in some kind of a picture or something. Then as everybody sits around a circle, you have to explain it and show and tell. I always had a hard time. I was just about five years old. I just lived through it.

It persisted all the way through high school and even into college. The worst thing is when you're an adolescent and you're in a classroom with other adolescents. They will make fun of you and they will imitate your mannerisms. Especially in my case where I started to develop some secondary physical symptoms such as physical shaking. Then you can see them out of the corner of your eye—see them shaking as you're standing up trying to recite an answer, shaking, too. Adolescents are the most unkind. As you get older, that is one problem that automatically takes care of itself. You're with a more mature group of people after you're out of high school.

Being called on in class is nonproductive

Sometimes I had an understanding with the teacher that he wouldn't call on me for any verbal work. I would be required to do the same tests and the other things. He just wouldn't bother to put me through that. I would appreciate when a teacher wouldn't call on me. Up until I was treated for the problem, there was no way I could control my stuttering. So there's always the constant anxiety when the stuttering gets out of control when you're before people. There's nothing effective, nothing regular and effective that you can do about it. That makes you more nervous and you stutter worse. Once when I was in eighth grade, I got yelled at for stuttering. I was told to just plain stop it. I thought that was insensitive and unkind.

How can you be accepted in high school? I don't know. I was never able to do anything about it, myself. The problem is, how do you get respect for yourself? It's mostly through words. That's the way we're trained. It was especially hard because I was in a private school. I was always in college prep courses with more intelligent students. Maybe somebody who has problems can be more charitable, more kind, than somebody who has everything to offer and thinks he can afford to laugh at other people. I would say the best thing is to try to make an arrangement not to be called on. If you aren't able to control your stuttering, what's the point in doing it over and over again as the stuttering gets deeper and deeper? You're not getting anything out of it. You're not training yourself. Just try to avoid having to speak and then try to get treatment. When you get treatment, then you ought to practice.

I didn't have a lot of anxiety about going to school. If I knew that I had to give a talk, then I did. My parents first thought it was an emotional problem, so I went to a counselor and talked about any problems I might have at home, any nervousness or anxiety. And it did help for a while. I would say for about a year or two. My stuttering had improved and I was able to talk before the class while I was in college. Yet for some reason, toward the end of my college years, it came back and it got worse and worse. All through graduate school.

While I was in graduate school, I went to visit an uncle in California. He had never met me. I stayed with him for a month. The first day he sat me down in the living room and started asking me questions. My stuttering was terrible. I felt so helpless, so far away from home with a stranger. I just felt terrible that first day. But he was nice about it and it improved. He just didn't make an issue over it. He suggested that I get some help. He said, "Why don't you try the University of Pennsylvania?" After I came back, that's what happened.

Basically a problem of rhythm

I went to the University of Pennsylvania to Dr. Brady. He didn't bother with counseling about my problems: "How do you feel about this?" or "How do you feel about that?" He just used behavioral treatment and that's what helped. His idea is that stuttering is basically lack of rhythm within a person's voice. By teaching a person to speak in rhythm you destroy the stuttering habit. He trains you to speak in a rhythm and for that he uses two general methods. He's developed a thing that looks just like a hearing aid and you wear it like a hearing aid, only instead of amplifying sound, it's a metronome. You hear a tick, tock, tick like you used to practice on a piano. By teaching yourself to say words with each tick, you put your speech into a regular rhythm. He supports that also by the fact that you can't stutter while you're singing a song.

He also uses the idea of putting a person on a mild tranquilizer. Some people have a very difficult time relaxing. One person in our group, even after using the thing in his ear, still stuttered terribly. Every single word was a long excruciating process for him. Dr. Brady kept putting him on gradually increasing doses of medication. I didn't see this person for a couple of months and when I came back, he was perfect. Talking, relaxed and fluent. So it was a combination of those two things. Plus he would use some slight aversion [therapy]. He would have you talk and practice before him, and if you didn't stick to the rhythm, he would have a flashbulb flash in your face as a mild punishment. You had to stop and start over again and keep yourself in rhythm all the time.

That was the first time I ever got regular help. And it's the regularity, the knowing that you've got something that will work, that makes you speak better. As long as you go through life knowing that it can start any time and you don't have any control over it, then you're in a constant state of agitation any time you have to speak.

There are funny patterns to the speech of a stutterer. A strange thing that I always notice, and I still don't understand, that when I'm really nervous, really wrapped up, really tense, I don't stutter that much. Stuttering tends to increase when I'm in a state of relaxation. That seems to be contrary to what Dr. Brady said, but still I found that out. If you're really harassed, under a lot of pressure, I think it takes your mind off the stuttering and you speak better. The other pattern is that people tend to stutter worse on the phone. When you're on the phone, the only part of you that shows through is your speech. They don't see your clothes, they can't see your height, they can't see anything about you, so on the phone, you're more on the line with that disability than at any other time. A part of Dr. Brady's training was to actually practice calling on the phone. He would have us call the airlines and make reservations or ask for information just to get the idea of practicing.

Right now, it isn't of any consequence

I'm a psychologist. If I had chosen my job on the basis of my stuttering I probably would not have chosen psychology because it's very verbal. I didn't seem to think about it at the time. You just think in terms of whether a job is interesting. At least in my case, when I was in high school and college, I didn't think of jobs in terms of practical things like, is there a market for it? How much is it going to pay? How much schooling will it take? Can I afford it? I didn't think about that. I had a lot of idealistic ideas.

There are occasions when I'll have trouble saying a few words, but generally there's no problem. Only once did I have a client who did poorly on a test say that my stuttering made him nervous. I think he was making excuses for not doing well. Right now, it isn't any consequence. I still feel tense when I speak before people. But I think if I worked on my rhythm more, that would help. I gave some small counseling courses. I spoke before people and I felt that tension. But I did it. I volunteered for it. I was told once by a teacher that stuttering would prevent a person from getting ahead. I never thought that it would.

I wasn't much of a social outgoing person, ever, but I don't think it was because of the stuttering. I was always working hard and studying hard. I always had a few friends in grade school and high school. I never thought of my stuttering as holding me back from things, though that might have been at the back of my mind.

Putting your worst foot forward

Some people, if they stop you on the street and ask you for directions, and you start to stutter, will just drive away and look like they're disgusted with you. I don't like people to step in when I'm having a block. Occasionally that happens and, though I appreciate their feelings toward me, the problem is that when somebody steps in, they might say the wrong thing. Then you not only gotta correct what they say, but then you gotta do it right. It only makes it more of a problem. If people would not try to supply the missing word, but just be kind and indulge you and maybe wait or say something nice to you, like, "Relax," that is more helpful than trying to fill in the blanks. That just makes everything more complicated.

If you're in line at the store and you start to stutter when asking for something, you feel like you're holding everybody else up. If they show they understand, that's enough. I don't feel there is anything that anybody can do more than that. What is irritating is if you say something and they don't understand it and then you have to say it again. You feel like, "Why don't you take my problem into consideration? Why are you so clumsy when here I am stumbling?" That is an irritation.

Brady used to give the MMPI to all the people who applied for his program. That's the Massachusetts Multi-phasic Personality Inventory. He told me that, as a general rule, stutterers have a poor self-image. That's a general trait that he saw. It could be that you have a poor self-image, then you stutter, then the stuttering makes you think less of yourself. Stop to think about all the ways that people try to make themselves look good—by haircuts and clothes and washing themselves. But so much comes through in your speech. That's probably more important than any part of you. That's the same if you were forced to walk around in rags or half naked. You would naturally feel self-conscious all the time. Stuttering has the same effect. You're always putting your worst foot forward when you speak, so you're always getting reinforced to think that, at the very least, you're an inept person compared to other people. It's hard.

People can't just look at stuttering as simply a behavioral thing. There's a tendency, even among stutterers themselves, to start ascribing other things to it, like more attributes. If a person stutters, you automatically say, "He's shy. He's an inept person. Maybe he's a cowardly person." There's a tendency not to confine your reasoning just to the stuttering. You start making all these unwarranted assumptions. I don't think the stutterers have as big an organization as the epileptics or the deaf or the blind. Stuttering makes you more alone in a sense.

I never blamed any person for my stuttering. Being a religious person, when I have problems, I can sometimes thank God for things he does. But I can be angry at him, too, because I think he's controlling everything. I have that faith. I sort of feel, "Why can't he help me?" I felt that way during the periods when it was severe. The only answer I have been able to think of is that stuttering, like any other problem, is God saying, "Let's see how you cope with it." Like poverty, like low intelligence, like a broken leg—let's see what you can do with it. Can you prove yourself?

George's message. I would advise parents to consider all avenues. I do think there is a psychological aspect to it, but I think the most important thing is that if a child can learn to physically speak, it will help him with some of his psychological problems. First find out if it can be behaviorally treated. Then if he has other problems, by all means explore them. Maybe counseling would help in that type of situation. There are also groups like the group I was in. Over and above the treatment we got, we would have social groups where we could learn how each of us felt about this particular problem. We would also practice reading plays and stories. That's a help. If you can talk to people with the same problems that you have, that's a good idea.

Don't be punitive because that's not going to help. It's only going to make it worse. Just let them know that you understand that you're not expecting them to say everything right all at once. That's about all you can do other than to guide them into a program like I was in.

APHASIA

JANET (A Volunteer)

Janet has aphasia as a result of a stroke. She describes her aphasia: "My situation is that what I think in my mind doesn't come out of my mouth."

My aphasia was complete for about two weeks. I couldn't talk at all. The first words I said were, "I love you," to my husband. For a long time I couldn't speak in sentences, only one word or two words. The same two words over and over. No matter what anybody said, I said the same thing repeatedly because that's all I could say. It was one year before I could speak in sentences at all and another year with speech therapy. Then I talked pretty much the same way I talk today but slower. Very much slower. Still sometimes I talk really nice and sometimes I can't describe in sentences what I think in my mind.

Even now I still don't know what happened to me. Even after five and a half years, I don't know what happened to me exactly. Nobody tried to help me understand my stroke. The doctors are so busy that I didn't want to bother them. The speech therapists asked me questions, but didn't tell me anything. Didn't offer me anything. They didn't tell me anything except when I asked. Those days I *couldn't* ask. All along, I was anxious to know and I couldn't get the right words out to ask somebody. With stroke victims, if they're not with it, you can talk and they won't listen anyhow. But if they are with it, they're gonna want to know. Sooner or later, they want to know what the limitations are. You don't want to say anything to discourage them, but tell them a little bit about it.

When I first realized I couldn't talk, I was mixed up, disturbed, and depressed. I thought I would always be that way. I didn't know that aphasia is something that gets better. That's why now I go to the hospital and tell other aphasia patients they can get better. Nobody came to me. I thought it was permanent. Three weeks later when I got speech therapy, that's when they told me I could talk. But for three weeks I didn't know whether I would ever talk or not. So it's important to communicate with the patient. I could understand, but I couldn't talk. If the patient knows that aphasia won't last, they won't be so depressed.

I used to teach reading and now I can't teach—now I can't read at all. Big words I can figure out, but little words still make me lose my mind: *if, for, was, when*. I can figure out books, but it takes me a long, long time. I can't read the newspapers at all. At first I was terribly disappointed not to be teaching. Now I know I will never work again. For a long time I still wanted to work, but now I'm adjusted. I can't move my arm at all and I don't know what kind of work there is to do when you can't move your right arm and you can't speak well. I can't read and I can't spell. I work in the hospital one day a week and in the school library one day. And one day I go to Bible reading. I can't read, but I can listen and that means a lot to me.

Now I listen

I am still self-conscious. For two or three years I was very uncomfortable when I spoke. I still say, "I am aphasic," before I speak. That clears the air. I have become quiet. Before I had aphasia, I talked constantly. Now I listen. It's easier to listen than talk. Especially if I say something and it doesn't come out the right way. Then I get mixed up. I get flustered very easily.

It's easiest with old friends. But with more than two or three friends, it's very frustrating. I can't describe or tell something to anybody exactly. I have to go all around the thing. People could help me a little bit. I can't speak and I know what I have in mind. I think the other person has an idea of what I want to say and they can speak for me. Just help me a little with one or two words. Then I can get the rest of the thing, move on, instead of agonizing to get the word out.

I can't read at all. It was many months before I found out about talking books. I was angry I didn't find out about them sooner. The sister at the School for the Blind told me about them six months after I had the stroke. Aphasia patients must be told about the books for the blind and then they have the option to get them or not. It meant a whole lot to me.

I'm closer to God and that's a big thing. Before I had the stroke, I was teaching and there were too many things happening in my life. Then I had the stroke and it removed a lot of it from my life. I got closer to God—less distraction.

I was teaching children who were lower functioning. Having the stroke helped me because now I am lower functioning, too. In his way, I understand their problems better. Before, I said to myself that you didn't learn because you didn't listen. Now I know that you don't learn because something's wrong with your head—not because you're lazy.

Janet's message. My message is to love people. And really get to know them. Accept them as they are.

7. SIZE
Reach Out for What's Inside

The kingdom of heaven is within you; and whosoever knoweth himself shall find it.
—Greek Papyrus

"How's the weather up there?" Such an inane comment.
—Steve

He is taller by almost the breadth of my nail than any of his court, which alone is enough to strike an awe into the beholder.
—Gulliver's Travels

SIZE

*Tall, Short,
Overweight*

Few people feel their bodies are perfect. Most people consider themselves too thin, too short, too fat, too tall. The condition becomes socially handicapping when the person involved *thinks* it is, or when he actually receives reactions such as stares, jokes, and even discrimination.

The advice to society is not to indulge in expression on the size or shape of the body, such as, "My, you're tall!" When you stand 6′ 8″, that is hardly news. Also emphasized was that our interaction with people should not be determined by arbitrary standards of physical normalcy. "Generally I want to get across to people that size and shape has nothing to do with you as a person" (Sara).

TALL

RICK (A Consultant)

Rick is 6' 8". His main problems are finding shoes to fit and people who won't stop making comments on his height.

I was aware I was taller probably from early grade school. My parents are both fairly tall so this was nothing negative. Being taller and physically bigger than a lot of other kids may have affected my personality. I was always pretty easygoing and tried to avoid a lot of conflicts in case people would say, "Well, you beat up on somebody because you're twice his size." I purposely tried to avoid a lot of contact with that type of person through both early adolescence right up through high school. It just made me ... I guess I shouldn't use the word "withdrawn." I was always pushed around a little bit more when making decisions with a group of friends. "What do you want to do?" "I don't really care. Whatever you guys want to do."

I was pretty much active in sports from my early childhood days: track, football, basketball—mainly those three. I enjoy most of 'em and not just because of my size. My father and friends all enjoy them. I didn't excel because I wasn't completely devoted to any one sport or sports as a whole. I always enjoyed sports for the recreational aspects—the physical satisfaction of feeling good more than trying to be excellent at any one sport.

People say I must be good at basketball and I still hear that now. I just accept it as something that people automatically say whenever they see somebody that's a foot taller [than most people]. They immediately think that you're a basketball player. My answer now to them is that I'm too old for that. And I hear, "Wow, you're tall." You hear that so much. I just comment on what they say and don't expound on it a great deal. I don't take it negatively at all. Except for the people who will stand there and continue to make comments about the weather and some comments which I've heard too many times over and over. It does get tiring.

I don't look at somebody and say, "Wow, you're short." It seems to me that most comments are made to tall people and that must mean that people don't think it's bad and maybe they're jealous. Otherwise, they wouldn't make those comments. I've never felt bad about being tall, or felt deprived. There are some pitfalls to it, but from a psychological viewpoint, I've never resented it.

Pitfalls

One of the pitfalls for me is buying clothes. I've always envied people who could walk into any store and get something on sale. Up until the last four or five years, it's been pretty tough for me to do that. Sale items—there are just not that many of them. Financially, it's hard to buy clothes and pay the full price especially when you wear suits and sport jackets and ties and dress shirts. Up until recently in a tall men's shop you went in and you got your choice of five suits in your size— maybe. But recently it's gotten a lot better, whether that's because there are more tall people or they just recognize a greater need for it.

When I'm in a clothing store a lot of time I'll wish I was six inches shorter. Same thing with my feet. Usually when you're tall, you have bigger feet so your selection of shoes is limited. I wear size 15. Up to size 13 is what most stores carry. So it's either out of a catalog or in a few select stores. I usually don't have any interest in going to a mall, shopping with the family. It's hard for me to even browse through a store because there's nothing there to even interest me. Even in buying a car, I'm limited. I can't go in and say, "I'd like this car because of the color and the price." I've gotta first sit in it and see if I feel comfortable. I had a Volkswagen, but the way it's built there was plenty of room. But right now there's probably not a foreign car that I could drive.

Beds—same thing. At home you don't have to purchase beds that often. You buy a bed and fit it with sheets. But staying in motel rooms or dormitories at college, beds do present a problem for a person my size.

Most doorways are 6' 8" so I can usually slide right under. Although people have told me that I do tilt my head a little bit out of habit because if I'm bouncing just right I can catch the top of the doorway. So I would say the physical inconveniences are the biggest drawbacks.

There are times that you feel a little bit self-conscious standing in a group when you don't know anybody and you kinda stick out because you're a head taller than other people. You would *feel* a little more uncomfortable. I wouldn't run and hide in a corner. But you still get the feeling that you are different than the rest of the crowd because you are taller.

People's reactions probably bring it to my attention more than anything else. You can tell if people are looking at you. It's pretty hard to whisper to somebody in the elevator: "I wonder how tall that guy is?" I work on the fifth floor and I'm in an elevator four or five times a day, so that's the area where people are just kind of standing looking at each other. On the street, you're past them and when you get past them they may make a comment or something.

What bothers me most is when people keep going and keep making comments—after a while this gets a little bit old. They usually don't do it if they're by themselves. It's usually with a group so maybe it's a way of impressing the group.

Rick's message. If I were talking to other tall people growing up, coming out into the world, I would say, "Try to be yourself." I've mentioned that I'm less aggressive. I don't know whether that's my personality and maybe I would be that way if I were 5' 9" or 6' 8". I would tell people that if they have a tendency to be somewhat aggressive, don't let their height stand in the way. I think that aggression is a good trait if it's used right—whether it's athletics or trying to get ahead or with your family in terms of leading them the right way. There are certain areas where aggression is good. I would say if there's a tendency to be that way, just be yourself and lead the life as you see fit.

If I were talking to society in terms of how they should feel toward tall people, it would simply be that tall people don't feel differently toward anybody else, so there's no reason that other people should feel any differently toward us.

STEVE (An Engineer)

Standing 6' 6" tall, Steve is a slender young man in his twenties.

Usually people don't think about tallness as an issue in their lives. Now and then it comes up. But you don't normally dwell on it. People who are neither particularly tall nor particularly short are more apt to think of it as something that must be important, instead of viewing it simply in terms of practicality and impracticality.

Most of the impact on a day-to-day level is little stupid, practical things. Mostly architectural problems. Getting one's head and one's feet on the bed at the same time. That's a problem. I have a 6 × 7 ft. water bed. It's an indulgence. But I get on there heel to toe and do not hit the edges.

Kitchen counters are always just too low and so you have to bend over to do everything. That makes your back hurt—especially when your back is real long. You can't wash your face without getting water all over everything because the sink is down around your knees somewhere. Of course, seating—there's never enough room for knees. And door closers that hang down on the inside of the door frame—those big hydraulic ones. I always thought that was a dumb idea.

I wouldn't want to be an inch taller because right now I can buy standard size 12 shoes. No problem. They're everywhere and they fit. If I needed a 13, it would be a real problem. I can buy a regular shirt. The sleeves aren't too short. I can buy jeans that are 36 inches long and they're fine. So I'm right at the end of all standard, mass manufactured sizes. That's great. *But no more, please.*

There are some advantages. Walking down the street, you see over people's heads—see where you're going. In a crowd, you're less apt to feel you're in a crowd because at least you can see around you. I can imagine what it would feel like if you were down there between everybody's shoulders. Just a wall of people around. It's nice to be able to reach things off high shelves. Look over walls.

How's the weather up there?

Most of the time I won't answer people when they ask, "How's the weather up there?" It's such an inane comment. It's supposed to be funny. It's just dumb. But it's benign. Nothing is meant by it. People usually say it with sort of a smile. If I'm feeling particularly kind toward humanity, I appreciate it as being at least better than nobody saying anything at all. Other times it is just an irritation—like I don't want to be bothered by these people.

When people look up at me and ask if I played basketball, I look down at them and ask if they played croquet. I wasn't on the basketball team. I was never very athletic. I found most of the atmosphere of athletics kind of repulsive. I thought it was unrealistic that people would think I would want to play basketball simply because I'm tall.

Somebody might have particularly nimble fingers and they don't have people running up to them, saying, "Hey, you really should be putting together ships and bottles. Wouldn't you like to? Here, have a bottle. Go ahead." It would make sense for a basketball player to be tall. It doesn't make sense for a tall person to necessarily play basketball.

Sometimes I would like to blend into the woodwork—observe a situation but not be involved in it. We all have our ways of doing that—leaning against the wall, slouching a little. There's a fellow at work who's very short—five and a half feet or something like that. When we stand next to each other just talking, it's sort of awkward. He stands up real straight and I kind of lean against the doorway. We manage to get about six inches out of the difference that way. We've caught ourselves doing that. We joke about it.

Throughout your life you're always standing out like a sore thumb. Whether you mean to or not, you command attention by just standing there—simply because you can't really not notice someone who is standing there six and a half feet tall. I think having a little bit of attention drawn to you all the time makes you more aware of how to cope with that, how to use that, how to take advantage of that.

There seems to be an idea—in fact, it's well documented—that people seem to give preferential treatment to tall people. I've read of studies where they tell you that out of so many people hired for various jobs with equal qualifications, all else being equal, the tall person often gets the job. There is a slight intimidating effect that tallness has. There's something about looking up to someone that seems to put you in a lesser position. People tend to react in some sort of animal level of functioning in which that is a form of domination. It's a very superficial reaction.

It's not really that much of an issue to me. Somehow I get the impression that people have a misconception. They think, "It must be great to be that tall!" or "It must be awful to be that tall!" Well, it's not a whole lot one way or another. It's just a minor advantage, probably. There isn't a whole lot to it.

SHORT

ANN
(A Medical Technologist)

Ann is five feet. She feels the world is geared to taller people.

I don't run into many people shorter than I am. Occasionally I run into somebody who's about the same size as I am and I think, "Wow, they're really small," and then I realize ... [laughs], they're probably a little taller than I am.

I suppose I've always been on the petite side. I prefer "petite" rather than "short." I didn't grow since I was fifteen when I was a freshman in high school. I was the shortest one in my class. In the class yearbook I was "the shortest girl." It's not a plus. It's not something you can put on your college résumé. It's not like something you achieved. It tends to be negative.

My parents were short, small. I inherited my size. I never felt bad about it. One disadvantage of being short is when you are dating: you probably end up with the shorter dates—shorter in stature.

I am a medical technologist. Something I noticed when I went through training is that the world is geared for taller people. I sometimes have difficulty reaching for instruments. If I have to prepare an instrument, I find myself having to stand on chairs. One centrifuge I used a great deal at the blood bank, I have to stand on my toes to look down to balance it. A couple of times I've turned around and it hasn't been balanced because I'm not able to see another tube that's down in the centrifuge that someone else has forgotten to take out. I'm just not *tall* enough to see down into it like everyone else can.

You lack authority

It's not just a job-related thing. It doesn't matter if you're in a store speaking to a salesman, or someone is coming into your house selling you something, or if you have a workman that you are dealing with—I think you lack authority when you're diminutive in stature. It's also a personality thing. Something that I say or do indicates that I'm "easy." Probably sometimes I'm aggressive just to prove myself.

Being short puts you at a disadvantage, particularly at a stand-up party. It's more difficult to converse with people. Most people are up here [points two feet up] and it's a little hard to talk to them. You *feel* awkward. I often feel ill at ease. It is also personality [problem], not necessarily stature, but *that* doesn't help.

Some people have come and said to me, "You're short." It's not an unusual reaction, but I don't enjoy it. I say, "Yeah, I've always been short. Ever since I was born I was short." But it annoys me. In fact, it annoyed me more after I read a "Dear Abby" column that said it was rude.

If I ever feel bad about being short, I think of that saying, "I cried because I had no shoes until I met a man who had no feet." My father was shorter than I—he was 4′ 11″. He was a hunchback and had a corresponding pidgeon breast. Living with his pain, it was nothing to be short.

Ann's message. Just don't sit in front of me at the movies!

PETER
(A Biologist)

Peter, a man in his mid-twenties, is 5' 3". I saw Peter walking down the street and asked if he would discuss his experiences and perspectives on being shorter than the norm in our society. Peter is employed as a biological research technician. He completed college and plans to work a couple of years before returning to school for a graduate degree. He considers himself an overachiever.

I was always the shortest person in the class. I stopped growing sometime in high school. You get garbage for it. If you weren't short, it would be something else. Everyone's got something. When people make wisecracks, if it's funny, I'll laugh. If you just get somebody being ignorant and stupid and they can't think of an articulate way to do it, then it's like "big deal." If it's humorous, I'll laugh. I do the same thing to lots of people and I hope that they laugh. It's not so much me personally. It could be any short person.

It was usually people much taller than I who would say something. I usually discounted it because I figured if that was all they had on me, then they didn't have a lot. I'm very articulate, so sometimes I'd beat them to death verbally. "Well, if that's the best you can do, tough, because I've obviously got you covered on all these other bases." And that shut them up. They challenged you and you didn't lose your cool and start yelling at them and being irrational. You just dealt with it. They would cool out.

There are ways to compensate

There are more ways to compensate. You do things a little harder—more intense. I'm an overachiever. That was the main defense, to overachieve. I was student council representative and then I became vice-president, then president. I was in wrestling. I was champion. Wrestling was one of those things where they weight-class us. You didn't have to be big. You didn't have to compete with 200-pound guys. I was academically achieving, too, so that I wasn't a "mini-jock."

People discount me because I'm short and they say, "Oh, you can't be serious." That will happen not only in a physical situation, but also in negotiations. You walk into a room and they size you up. They make an immediate impression of you. Primarily because you're short, they think they have something on you. What you generally do is don't address that issue directly because they think you're very defensive about it and they have, in fact, found a weak point. What you do is just sidestep it and let them take you for granted: open up a weak spot and exploit it. Just win that point in negotiation. I had a very expansive personality, in fact, bigger than life. That was how I got through a lot of things.

I never thought of myself as really being short until I got to college. People in Puerto Rico where I grew up tend to be shorter. I'd never run into situations where size per se was the problem. Even now, when I'm looking at other people on the street who I think are roughly my size, they tend to be people who are four or five inches taller than I am. It's like I have a much more expanded physical image than reality. I'm always very surprised when I see myself in the mirror next to somebody who is over six foot. I think the disparity is incredible.

People who don't see me for a while will say, "Oh, boy, you seem shorter." People who meet me when I'm sitting down will say when I stand up, "Oh . . ." or people who have seen pictures of me say I have a face of a taller person.

I think when it hit me that I was shorter was in the area of dealing with women. Some taller women really get very hyper about height and that's an issue in their mind as well as mine. I was going out with this one woman. I guess she was about 5' 10" We broke up over the summer when unbeknownst to me she was going out with someone else.

There wasn't a whole lot to this guy. The only thing I could figure was he was someone taller than I was. That was when I really began to confront my height. I collapsed. I became withdrawn for a couple of months. I had to begin building right back up again. There was a period when, I guess, subconsciously, I was just going with tall women. I found them attractive. I guess psychologically, I was thinking, *"Well, I might be short but I'm not a little guy."* But you walk down the street with a woman eight inches taller than you are, you're gonna get remarks.

Snap judgments
If I were to go into business, I would have a tremendous amount of difficulty because the initial impression of a little guy is to discount him. You look at the kinds of people who are successful in business and they tend to be tall—very large. It's totally based on appearance. In that sense it would be very difficult for me to go into business.

There's always going to be somebody making a snap judgment and underestimating me. The big problem is when they realize they're underestimating me and then they overcompensate, overestimate. They decide that I'm overly competent, so they relax: "He's more than competent." Then you make a mistake because you can't keep that constant level of performance. It sort of shuffles back and forth until they find some kind of middle ground.

There are a few stereotypes of short people that are paradoxical. One is "Center of Attraction. Joker." Another is "The Wimp" who is totally ineffectual. The third is "The Little Napoleon Syndrome"—you have to go out and conquer. Depending on how you mix them, you get whatever you want.

Short people tend to be taken less seriously. That presents a problem because when you want to come across as serious, you aren't believed. There's no credibility. I related to that problem in college where I got a reputation for being a clown. When you get that kind of reputation, you can't sell somebody a serious idea. At the back of their minds, they're thinking, "There's some kind of joke coming." As people get to know you, they realize you're a multifaceted character. I wouldn't mind being taller. If I grew another six inches, it wouldn't hurt.

Peter's message. How should you treat short people, handicapped people, black people, women, oppressed minorities? There are so many levels of discrimination. The most important, fundamental ones are the economic, political ones. So some people down the road don't like me—big deal! That's not the problem. The problem is when you can't get a house, a job, or an education.

OVERWEIGHT

SARA
(An Occupational Therapist)

Sara is 5' 9" and approximately 100 pounds overweight. She is a young attractive married woman with one child. She would like to have more children, but not until she loses weight.

I wasn't overweight until I got into the third grade. You become pretty much aware. Children are very honest. Plus, in my school we had a program where we were weighed and measured every report card. It was done by teachers, not nurses. Sometimes they made sarcastic remarks about how much I gained. Sometimes they were more considerate. I wasn't a lot overweight. I was just very big.

I was teased by kids. I coped by being funny, by laughing at myself. The teachers laughed along with the kids. I can't remember any who intervened. I wish they had—if they had handled it right. If they didn't, it would be worse. It's a stereotype that people who are fat are jolly. And I fit right into that stereotype. It worked and they didn't tease me anymore. They acted toward me as someone who's funny—who's fun to be with. It got tiresome. People tend to think you have no feelings. That they can play every joke on you because you're a good sport. It ended up being a vicious circle. They didn't tease me anymore about being overweight, but now they pulled a lot of pranks on me because I was a good sport.

I guess a teacher could've explained in health class that there are norms and there are differences. That people have different health problems, metabolic rates, whatever. Make the kids aware that not everybody's the same. No one ever said to me, "You might be different than her, but that's okay, because she's not necessarily normal. She's not the standard you have to measure up to."

I had dates, but they were more on a friendly basis. I dated very seriously my senior year when I had lost quite a lot of weight. Because of the stereotypes or because of the norms that are set up by our society, men tend not to be attracted to women who are overweight. You don't see fat women in magazines. You become more self-conscious, not always having a date compared to a lot of your friends. But I always got reinforced from my folks that I was a nice person. It didn't always make me feel much better, though.

The world revolves around food

I've had thyroid testing. My grandmother had a thyroid condition. I supposedly don't, but I have a very low metabolic rate. I can only lose on a day's calories of 900 to 1000. It's the only way I can lose large amounts of weight and I've lost 70 to 80 pounds at a time. I've lost large amounts and I gain it back over time.

I'm 60 pounds lighter than I was in 1980, but I have to lose about 100 more and that's large numbers. Weight-watchers is the best diet. I haven't tried anything but Weight-watchers and Tops. I'm not one for trying freak diets.

When you think about it, the whole world revolves around food. Every occasion we have, there's a special food for it. First thing people say is, "Let's have a party. What food will we bring?" When you're on a diet, you don't feel you can go anywhere, to anyone's house. If you don't eat what's on the table, it insults the person who invited you. You have to be a very strong person. Obviously, I haven't been all the time or I would have stuck it out.

Judging by appearance

I did experience prejudice getting my first job. It was an obstacle. In addition, we didn't have a lot of money, so I didn't have really nice clothes. It makes it very hard when you're overweight—clothes are more expensive. You could definitely tell just the way people talked or the way they acted, they were judging by appearance.

When I first meet anybody, they're very standoffish. It's almost as if I have to prove myself as a person or as a professional before I'm accepted. That's a drag. But once I've been able to get across to someone that I'm a person, then I'm usually accepted.

The only time I really get overt reactions is from older people or from children because they're very straightforward or from people who are prejudiced. They couple being overweight with being out of control of the rest of your life. Like it's something that's across the board—it's part of you. You can't hide it. You can hide a lot of other strange things about yourself.

Right now is the most difficult part of my life. My weight's a problem because I want more children and it's frustrating to me. I really want to have more kids. My husband was upset after I had my child and gained weight. I think he appreciated my figure more when I was slender. I'm sure of it. I can't put myself in his place, but I get messages the way he reacts. I think it would be handled better if he'd just be forward and forthright as opposed to not trying to hurt my feelings. I would appreciate his just leveling with me, but he isn't the type of person to be cruel about anything.

My daughter is the most supportive person in my life when I go on a diet. She tends to be kind of a pain, but she's a very good watchdog. She knows I will not have children while I'm overweight and she really wants brothers and sisters and she's all for it.

Sara's message. Teach your child. Teach your child how to ration. Teach them what a good balanced meal is and why it's important. Don't have a lot of junk [food[around the house. My mom didn't like to cook so things that were fast were available periodically. She allowed us to have snacks and stuff. I think children should all be taught moderation, for anyone can develop a weight problem later on, too. If they develop bad eating habits, as they get older they could start putting on the weight. My daughter is constantly hounding me for snacks and treats and I don't have anything around for treats unless it's a special occasion. I usually have raisins and apples and bananas and yogurt and cheese and sugarfree gum. She thinks I'm a tyrant.

Children can learn in school about the psychological aspects of how people feel. They could try to role play people's feelings, helping children learn by real experiences as opposed to just reading and writing about them. It's got to start young.

I've worked with so many disabilities—no legs, no arms, no brain function—you name it. I've worked the gamut and every person I've worked with is different in his or her own way no matter what the disability. Working with the disabled has made me a stronger person in a lot of ways. So many disabled people are so much better than people who have all their abilities intact. I've decided that maybe they're more normal because they can adapt. They're the survivors compared to the people who are not open-minded and tend to be prejudiced. Generally I want to get across to people that size and shape has nothing to do with you as a person.

BONNIE
(A Sign Language Interpreter)

Bonnie is 5' 8" and weighs over 200 pounds. She is an interpreter for the deaf by training and an Irish dancer by avocation, so she is often in the public eye. Bonnie is now working as a houseparent for mentally retarded, hard of hearing adults.

I have a weight problem. I weigh over 200 pounds. A good weight for me would probably be about 160 because I'm tall. Anyone that is fat is prejudiced against because of their weight. You don't even necessarily have to be too fat or obese. In some circles, even if you're slightly pudgy, you're overweight. Also it depends on how you feel inside about yourself. You can be ten pounds overweight and still have a weight problem because you can't drop those ten pounds and you don't feel comfortable with yourself. *You don't feel you're worth much because of your overweight problem.*

It is not so much which word you use—pudgy, chubby, fat, or obese—as how that person is feeling about how much they weigh. Obese is really pretty heavy. Obese—that's your label. Maybe you're not an entity. Maybe you're not a person because obese is there first.

My mother has been heavy her whole life. She always thought she didn't want her daughter to be heavy. I basically have fat genes. I've a predestination for being overweight. I have been up and down the scales most of my life. I don't have a wardrobe. The age I am now I should have nice clothes, but every year I'm a different weight.

I was a fat child. It wasn't until sixth grade that I was aware of being fat. I don't know if it was because of puberty or because I changed schools at that time. Up to that time I accepted myself for whatever I was. I had gone to a parochial school. You wore a uniform a certain size. Other people didn't wear that size. It was not a big thing. When I moved to the suburbs and public schools, that really started a lot of things happening. You got weighed. You went to the nurse. "Why are you fat?" They put you on a diet. That's when my mother started taking me to doctors and giving me pills and *I began the whole accordion cycle* that my whole life has been.

We also had class pictures. You see yourself among all your skinny friends. That's when it really strikes you in the face—when you have to look at it.

When I hit twelve or thirteen, everyone was very weight conscious. In public school you had to take gym. You had to wear shorts and run around and try to kick the ball the farthest. In some ways I hated gym because I couldn't do everything. Also the embarrassment of wearing shorts or not fitting properly into your little gym uniform that everyone fit so well into. Not only was I fat, but I was tall and fat. You should be short and fat or tall and thin. You should never be tall and fat. Ever. So being uncomfortable was one of the main reasons I didn't like gym. All those skinny little classmates were running around and kicking the ball and doing calisthenics.

I never had a date in high school. I didn't have a date until I was about nineteen and I lost about eighty pounds. Now that I look back I think a lot of it was the way I was raised with the attitude about myself. I was always up and down and taken to the diet doctors who gave me pills to make me thin for a year, then I'd go off them because they're dangerous, then I'd get fat. I was in and out all the time and my personality was never encouraged to develop. *I was brought up feeling fat was first and person was second, so the person got lost in the fat.* Even when I was a thin person, I was still confused about who I was.

I went to one diet doctor and lost about eighty-five pounds. I got down to about a size twelve which is pretty thin for me. I was thin for ninth and tenth grades. Then I had to stop going to him because my brother went to him and landed in the hospital. So my mother took me off those pills and I gained all that weight back, plus more pounds . . . in one year. I was like a rubber band going in and out of clothes.

My senior year I decided I was going out for clubs. I was in about four clubs so my picture was all over the yearbook—unfortunately. I was in the Pep Club and in the Bowling Club. I found out from bowling that you really have to be in some kind of shape to bowl—even to *bowl*. I injured a finger, my thigh muscles, just because I was out of shape totally.

I *will* always *have a weight problem*

Even tomorrow, if I woke up thin, I would still have a weight problem because it's been ingrained in me for so long. The only reason I'm probably able to do this interview without breaking down or running away is because I've joined Overeaters Anonymous—which is a wonderful club. They help you accept who you are *right now*. You will get thin sooner or later, but they help you accept who you are right now.

I work with handicapped, mentally retarded, hearing impaired adults as a houseparent. It is supporting me through going to school, but I do enjoy my job. I am going to school to become an interpreter for the deaf. Being an interpreter you have to accept yourself and the way you look because you have to be able to use your body for getting another language across to a deaf person. You use body language and you use facial expression. I had a real icy jolt because we have to use video tape. The first time I saw a video tape of myself, I really could not handle it. I was very upset. Video tapes make everyone look terrible! If you're short, you look shorter, if you're fat, you look fatter, if you have a big nose, it looks bigger. Video tape can really destroy you. The first year in the program I really had a hard time dealing with it. I did go into Overeaters Anonymous and they helped me accept where I am now so I can look at a video tape and say, "I *did* that terribly, didn't I?" There's a big difference between saying, "Boy, I look fat on that tape," and "Boy, I did a lousy job." When I first looked at it, all I could see was the fat. It's progressed to where I am looking at my work instead of my appearance—which is a miracle in itself.

There is weight discrimination. There definitely is. If you go for a job, they'll find some reason not to hire you and it's probably your weight. Today in the job market, if you're going to hire someone and there are ten applicants for the job and there's one who's overweight, that person's going to get kicked off right away just because of whatever cockamamy stories that they believe about weight. You're an insurance risk or you might have to go out on disability. Why don't they say a skinny person could have a nervous breakdown?

Most of the time I've been able to accept myself. If you want to say, "You're fat." I'll say, "Good, I know that." I realize that. Let's go on from there. I have to carry around these extra pounds. You're not carrying me around. You only have to look at it. You should have to live with it. I get very tired of the word "willpower."

Who says that to you?

Skinny people. I'll usually throw back at them such as, "Do you smoke?" I mean, you have some vice, and I'll find out what it is and then I'll tell you to use willpower and stop it.

At Overeaters Anonymous I found out that many people are allergic to food such as white flour and white sugar, which is one of my problems. But right now I can't afford to eat properly. You can get, for example, a meatball sandwich and a soda from a vendor for $1.70. You go and get a healthy sandwich and a soda and it's going to cost you $3.

Believe it or not, I do not eat four hoagies for lunch. I look like I eat four hoagies for lunch, but I do not. I eat a normal portion, but with my system and eating white flour and white sugar, I gain the weight. I think I'll always feel that people think I eat a lot. I don't eat *that much*, but I look like I do and therefore people feel I must. In reality, the starches I eat go right on my hips where other people burn them up by running or just having an active metabolism. I don't feel guilty when I eat something that's wrong. I feel sad. I'm the kind of person who's going to have to carry around these pounds. But it's kind of sad why I can't stop doing this. I have to get myself back on the right track. But anyone who's overweight—it's *their* problem.

I took up jogging. At that time I thought I was pretty thin. I fit into a man's size large running shorts. I don't know if you think that's fat or thin for a girl. I was at one of my thinner periods. I was jogging, trying to tone up some of this flab I had, and I had kids saying, "Look at all that flab. I can't believe it!" I had just lost sixty or eighty pounds. I got very angry. I felt like saying, "Hey, what's it to ya?" But I didn't want to get stabbed so I just kept jogging away. I think people should shut up. *If you see somebody overweight jogging, applaud them.* They're the ones carrying all that weight on their sneakers. What do you care what they look like?

Recently I had to move. I was having an interview to get roommates. I thought, "Oh, my, it's like a job interview." I know I'm fat. People are going to look at me and say, "Oh, she's fat. I don't want her living here." But Overeaters Anonymous principles are still with me. They're ingrained. I started thinking, "How about if *I* don't want to live there?" This is normal thinking. This is the way I would teach my children. It's not the way I was taught at all. I was always taught they were gonna look at you as a fat person and you have to win them over. So I thought, let me see how I like this. And I felt so at home with the people. I did not feel fat the whole time I was there. When I came out, it was, "Hey, that was neat. I didn't feel fat." It was very hard to believe. It was a new experience. That was a very unusual happening and I hope it happens more and more.

I don't think I can blame anybody that I am fat. I did blame my mother for not encouraging me to become a person—to find that person inside of me. I get angry, sure. Why do I have this problem? It's a cross. Give the cross to someone else—let them carry the cross. Sure, I'd like to be thin.

I don't know if it has been a strength in my life, but it's helped me get in touch with a lot of sensitive people that I might not have. I might have been a skinny secretary all these years and never gotten in touch with what I've developed—such as working with the population that I do.

I would like to help other heavy people when I see them. I'd like to say, "Hey, there's hope. Go to this meeting." I never really had the guts to go up to someone and say, "Why don't you go to this meeting?" But if they ask me any questions about my losing weight, or going to any groups, I lead them into it. If someone came up to me and said, "You should be in this group," I'd say, "It's none of your business." If that person is ready to go into a group, they'll find it. They'll go to Weightwatchers, they'll go to a diet club, they'll go someplace. If they're not ready, your saying something to them is only going to push them further back.

Bonnie's message. Accept people as they are. If a person has a weight problem accept that person first as a person and let that person work on the weight. Don't see persons as fat people. Leave the fat alone. If they're overweight, they have to carry those pounds around; they know they're overweight. I don't see why it should bother other people. I would say, "Stop concentrating on the weight of that person and develop what's inside."

THE AUTHOR

Dhyan Cassie received her BA in English literature from Westminster College in New Wilmington, Pennsylvania, in 1957. After studying and working in the Middle East for four years under the auspices of the Presbyterian Church, she returned to Princeton Theological Seminary for special studies. She subsequently became a teacher of the deaf and earned her master's degree in audiology from the University of Pittsburgh.

She has worked in schools for the deaf in New Jersey, Rhode Island, Illinois, Puerto Rico, and Pennsylvania. In Puerto Rico she founded an audiology clinic in a Health, Education, and Welfare center in La Playa, Ponce.

Dhyan is now an audiologist at the Elwyn Nevil National Rehabilitation Center in Philadelphia where she works with the multiply handicapped and the elderly. She has written two other books and several articles in her field.

She is a member of Tabernacle Presbyterian Church, Philadelphia, Pennsylvania. Her husband is the associate executive for evangelism and social witness of the Presbytery of Philadelphia. They have two children, Giles and Andrea.